The Art of Writing Christian Poetry

Written By

Rev. John Marinelli

This book is published by Rev. John Marinelli. No portion of this book may be reproduced without the expressed written consent . Respond to johnmarinelli@embarqmail.com.

The Art of Writing Christian Poetry
is written by John Marinelli

1st edition…Copyright: 2003 by Rev. John Marinelli, P.O. Box 93345 Lakeland, Florida, 33804.

2nd edition copyright 2020 by Rev. John Marinelli P. O. Box 831413 Ocala, FL. 34483.

All rights are reserved.

Printed in the United States of America

Print I.S.B.N. 978-1-0878-5587-5
EBook I.S.B.N. 978-1-0878-5591-9

ACKNOWLEDGEMENTS

I would like to thank the following people for their help and encouragement:

1. My wife Marilyn for suggesting that I write this book and encouraging me to finish it. Also for her careful review and final edit.
2. My mother Lois Marinelli for doing the first edit and spell checking.
3. The Holy Spirit for Divine revelation and wisdom in the preparation and review process.

ABOUT THE AUTHOR

JOHN MARINELLI

Rev. Marinelli is married and the father of two grown children. He was the Co-Founder of the Fellowship of Christian Poets, a worldwide Christian ministry that is now operated by a friend. He is also the co- author of "Together Forever" a marital enrichment home seminar and author of "other books currently in the marketplace and offered on his website at www.christian;iferesourcecenter.org.

Rev. Marinelli is a bible teacher, poet and playwright. A biblical collection of his poems were displayed on three foot by four foot signs in the 250 acre nature sanctuary of Holy Land USA in Bedford, Virginia. Over the years, he has won several awards for outstanding poetry from other poetry groups, not currently in operation.

John and his wife, Marilyn are co-authors of, **"The Story of Jesus"**, an audio book CD set in musical poetry, currently being offered through www.christianliferesourcecenter.org.

John began writing poetry during college when he was assigned a writing task in his humanities class. He asked the Lord to help him compose a poem and off it went, a gifting and love for poetry that has never stopped. John has written over 300 love poems to his wife Marilyn, over 300 Christian poems on various subjects, more than 60 children's story poems, multiple biblical story poems and many seasonal holiday poems for family and friends.

John is not only an author, poet and playwright; but he is also an ordained minister. He has formed and been pastor of one church in Wisconsin and was the pastor of another in Alabama. He has also been a Youth Minister and Evangelism Director over the years. Currently, he ministers through his website and writes Christian Fiction books.

John's love for God and poetry has forged the way for other poets to gain self-confidence and to grow in their gifting. He strongly believes that poetry is a gift from God and feels that benefits from such a gifting is a divine privilege.

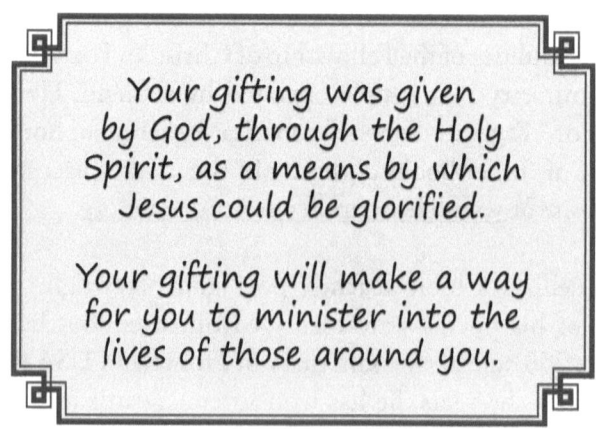

Your gifting was given by God, through the Holy Spirit, as a means by which Jesus could be glorified.

Your gifting will make a way for you to minister into the lives of those around you.

CONTENTS

Acknowledgements iii
About the Author v
Gallery of Poems ix
Introduction xi
Chapter 1.   The Christian Poetic Expression 1
Chapter 2.   What Is Christian Poetry? 6
Chapter 3.   Types of Christian Poetry 10
Chapter 4.   Profile of A Christian Poet 14
Chapter 5.   Recognition, Self-Worth And Poetry 18
Chapter 6.   Poetry, The Language of Love 25
Chapter 7.   Divine Inspiration 30
Chapter 8.   Poetry And Holy Spirit Conviction 37
Chapter 9.   Poetry In Motion 40
Chapter 10. Biblical Concepts And Poetry 54
Chapter 11. Writing Story Poems 63
Chapter 12. Building A Better Poem 69
Chapter 13. Are You Mocking God? 75
Chapter 14. Profitable Poetry 78
Chapter 15. Witnessing Through Poetry 83
Chapter 16. Getting Published 89

Chapter 17. Good Poetry A "How To" Review 93
Chapter 18. Walking Through The Titles 98
Chapter 19. Questions And Answers 102
Chapter 20. Resting In The Lord 110
Conclusion 115
Poetic Jargon 117

GALLERY OF POEMS

Listed below are original poems by the author that appear within various chapters. They are reflective of the types, styles and content of Christian poetry. The list is in order of their appearance.

For The Joy Set Before Me
With Earthen Vessels
With Eagle Wings
 Poet of the Lord
Wise Men Still Seek Him
I AM" There
 Fragile Flower Red
Holy Spirit
The Good Samaritan
The Angels Cry Holy
Agreeing With God
From Tears To Smiles
A Whisper in the Wind
A Gift From The God Of Eternity

Types And Shadows
In A Twinkle Of An Eye
The Pastor And The Master
Jonah And The Whale
Our Time of Prayer
There Is Still Time
God's Highway
Call Upon The Lord
The Way Maker
It Came To Pass
There Is No Other
A Love Poem From Jesus
Rest My Child

INTRODUCTION

"The Art of Christian Poetry" is a beginner's guide to understanding Christian poetry and its place in today's world. It is designed as a helpful tool in the discovery of one's poetic talent, source of inspiration and ministry value. I have added marketing and special ministry tips along the way as examples of some new and unusual ideas for the use of Christian poetry.

My source of knowledge comes from Divine revelation, biblical and secular study, writing poetry for over 30 years and review and editing of poetry as the Co-Founder and President of the Fellowship of Christian Poets. I do not presume to be the final "Say-So" or an expert in the field.

I support the traditional and basic teaching of how to write poetry. I have however, added a Christian perspective that will help the Christian beginner to understand his or her unique gifting and ministerial significance.

There are plenty of good books on the subject of writing poetry. My counsel is directed along the lines of being biblically sound, ministerial correct and what is acceptable to the suffering soul.

CHAPTER ONE

THE CHRISTIAN POETIC EXPRESSION

Inspirational poetry goes back to before the Old Testament prophets. In fact, according to Holman's Bible Dictionary, one third of the Old Testament is cast in poetry. Thirty-five Old Testament books contain poetic expressions that often include prophetic overtones.

From Genesis 2:23 through Zechariah 9-11:3, words of encouragement and religious instruction are evident. In some cases, as in most of the book of Isaiah, even future events are presented in poetry.

Prophecy and poetry have been teammates through the centuries. Their voices cry out to a lost and dying world. They speak to a troubled church. Both declare the majesty and glory of God.

It was the 1st century Christians, however, that led the way for modern Christian poetry. Their relationship with Jesus inspired their writings as they focused their attention on being in harmony with God. The result was an in-filling of love, joy, peace, compassion, and a host of other deep emotions that gave evidence of their love for God and their faith in Jesus Christ. Out of this inspiration came a poetic expression that we now call Christian.

This uniquely Christian expression was and still is characterized by three separate and distinct factors: **Co-Authorship, Christian Focus,** and **Spiritual Unity.** These are the building blocks of good Christian poetry.

Co-Authorship is the trademark of all Christian poetry. The inspiration comes from the same Holy Spirit that moved upon the prophets of old. However, this time, it's from an indwelling presence rather than an overshadowing anointing that fell only to depart again. The inspiration is from God and the style is from the poet. Together they form the content of the poetic expression.

Christian Focus: The focus of all Christian poetry is on the Christian experience through a personal relationship with Jesus Christ. The poet's inspiration is more personal in nature than even traditional secular sources. Instead of the beauty of a tree, it is the glory of the one that created the tree that inspires the poet.

Spiritual Unity is a two-fold process that involves both redemption and restoration. Both are central to the overall message. Both validate the inspiration as truly being from God.

This unique partnership in poetry quickly spread into the main stream of the Christian experience. Suddenly and without warning, Jewish and Gentile Christians began to express their most intimate and personal experiences with God through poetry. Slowly but surely, a "Christian Poetic Expression" emerged outside of its Hebrew origins into the entire Christian world.

As the "Christian Poetic Expression" became evident in all ethnic groups, its pulse was felt in poems of praise, prayer, prophecy, and thanksgiving. Its voice was heard through poems that edified, declared, revealed, and encouraged.

Christian poetry quickly became therapeutic in nature. It calmed the troubled soul; it strengthened weary hearts and fostered faith.

It offered comfort, blessings, guidance, encouragement, instruction, and even a gentle rebuke.

Many of today's Christian poets have their own Internet website and use computers as an every day tool to compose, edit and log their work. They come from all nationalities, all denominations, all walks of life, all ethnic backgrounds, and all age groups. Their poetry is an expression of the times in which they live. They author poems on anti-abortion, human rights, as well as, love, praise, faith and the other relational aspects of their Christian walk.

Today's Christian poets share their gifting as a ministry of love. Their ministries include; comfort to the elderly, sending poetic letters of protest to local newspapers, penning poetic tracts for the lost and greeting cards for various holidays. Some even design giant poster poems for public display.

The "Christian Poetic Expression" is very alive and well in today's world. It has survived the trials and tribulations of over 2,000 years and will continue until Jesus returns. Its future lies in the hands of countless thousands of Christians who seek and enjoy Divine Inspiration. Its value is as good as the poet's relationship with Jesus.

For The Joy Set Before Me

I could have lived forever,
As a simple mortal man.
I could have called 10,000 angels,
To help me to stand.
But I laid down my life
Despising the shame.
For the joy set before me,
Was your life to gain.

I could have stayed in heaven,
As the supreme ruler of all things.
I could have played among the stars,.
And listened for the flutter of angel's wings.
But I laid down my life,
Despising the shame.
For the joy set before me,
Was to know you by name.

I could have sent my armies,
To rid the world of sin.
I could have destroyed the earth,
As I did way back then.
But I bore the suffering of the cross,
Despising the shame.
For the joy set before me,
Was to take away your pain.

I could have done a lot of things,
To make this world right.
Or I could have done nothing,
And ignored your plight.
But God so loved the world,
That I endured the shame.
For the joy set before me,
Was your love to gain.

CHAPTER TWO

WHAT IS CHRISTIAN POETRY?

Let's first look at what Christian poetry is not.

1. It is not just poetry that was written by a Christian.
2. It is not the reflections of your personality or imaginations.
3. It is not humanistic, religious, political or secular.
4. It is not a forum or pedestal for the expression of "self."
5. It is not a quest into the painful past.

Most poetry in the world today is what we would call "secular" poetry, which is to mean, "non-Christian." I have a book published for children that is not Christian poetry and many poems about life that are not characterized as Christian.

Christian poetry has one key distinction that sets it apart from all other poetry. This distinction is the anointing of the Holy Spirit. Secular, religious, political and other poetry does not have this distinction. It is only given to Christian poets. I do not mean to say that other poems are not funny, good, or less in their expressions than anointed poems. I do mean to say that an anointed poem stands out and identifies itself as definitely Christian.

The anointing brings certain qualities to a poem. They include: The glory to God; attention to the name of Jesus; a ministerial message of hope and encouragement; the presence of God upon the reader. When a poem is anointed, the Holy Spirit breathes upon it. His Divine revelation is hidden within the words and imagery. It is always redemptive in nature.

Other characteristics include:

1. Up-lifting therapeutic messages that cleanse the soul and set the spirit free.
2. A symphony of thought that clearly reveals a co-authorship between God and man.
3. Praise and adoration towards Jesus for all that He has done.
4. Various styles of expression that are uniquely Christian such as: prophecy, prayer, biblical doctrines, praise, thanksgiving, etc.
5. A road map that leads the reader to a haven of rest where he or she is set free and edified.

Writing Christian poetry is a gift from God. I can't tell you how many poets have come my way saying that they had no real interest in poetry until one day when God just dropped it into their spirit. Most have little or no formal training, yet fashion poems that are power packed and oozing with the presence and glory of God.

That is not to say that the basic mechanics of good poetry are not relevant. They are! It just seems as though they overflow with the glory and presence of God and often still fill the mechanical requirements.

Is secular poetry then of no value? Of course not, it is still of value and can be enjoyed by friends, family and other poetry readers. However, you should never, ever search for sorrowful or painful experiences from the past as topics for fashioning a poem.

The enemy would love to lead you down a path where he can torment you and keep you dwelling on the past instead of going on with the Lord. Instead, write from your happy experiences or imagination that will bring joy and laughter to others.

In the final analysis, Christian poetry can be clearly distinguished by:

1. The Presence of God
2. The Anointing of God
3. The Glory of God
4. The Truths of God's Word
5. The Revelation Knowledge of God
6. The Power of God
7. The Peace of God

We should acknowledge that all of us write secular poems, as well as, those that are breathed upon by God. However, the secular usually does not fit in our ministerial environment.

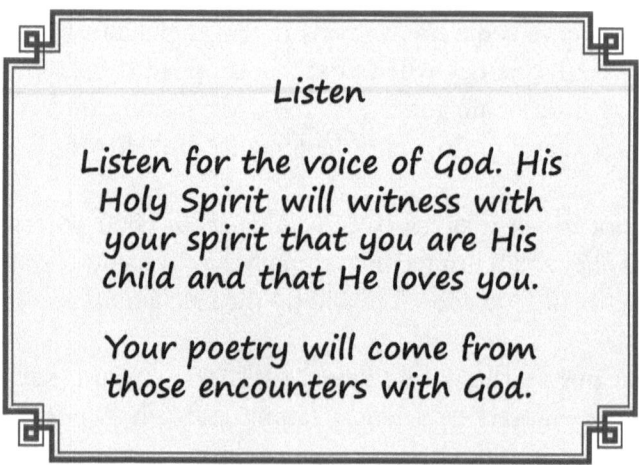

Listen

Listen for the voice of God. His Holy Spirit will witness with your spirit that you are His child and that He loves you.

Your poetry will come from those encounters with God.

With Earthen Vessels

Earthen vessels have never shown,
Such Glory that once was known.
Through time and all of eternity,
Came the Glory of His Majesty.

Full of love and full of grace,
He dwelt among the human race.
To heal the sick, the blind and the lame,
To free mankind from sin and shame.

With earthen vessel He conquered all,
By perfect obedience to His call.
For this we praise His holy name,
Full of grace and full of fame.

The Glory of His Majesty
Still shines through from eternity.
Again and again to meet life's call,
In earthen vessels to conquer all.

CHAPTER THREE

Types of Christian Poetry

When we speak of types of Christian poetry, we mean the categories or headings in which poems tend to gather. If you know all or most of the types, you can experiment with them in developing your skill.

Praise & Worship...This type of poem calls attention to the glory and majesty of God. It brings to the reader the awesomeness of God and the reality of His power, beauty, holiness and love. It primarily focuses on the attributes of God as a central theme.

Prayer & Petition...This type offers an intimate picture of the relationship between the believer and the Lord. Prayer poems can be conversational, petition or adoration. They can and often mix in praise, declaration, petition and faith.

Encouragement...There is nothing better than a word in due season, when the answer you seek is set before you. This type of poem is usually one of encouragement when the Lord comforts, strengthens, challenges, and heals the saddened heart.

Spiritual Warfare...This type of poem emphasizes the battle, the process and the weapons to accomplish victory. It often is a chant or faith declaration based upon the spoken word from the Bible.

Redemption...This type of poem includes the atonement, the cross, the sacrifice and all of the many ramifications that follows.

Evangelism...These poems focus on the call to salvation and the outreach to the lost. Also included are the concept of sin, forgiveness, and repentance.

Prophecy... A prophetic poem deals with the future. It will display the gifts of the Spirit in operation as a revelation to the poet or as a message to all who read.

Instruction...A poem of instruction is a "Thus Sayeth The Lord" that provides the reader with direction, truth and stability.

Exhortation...This type is the positive, full of faith, power packed gospel in a non-preaching yet ministerial manor that counsels, comforts, confirms, and convicts the reader.

Biblical Stories....About Biblical characters, events and happenings.

Celebrations...Including Christmas, Easter, and other Biblical celebrations.

Creation & Nature...This category reveals the handiwork of God in nature and the creation.

Biblical Doctrines...Including: The body of Christ, discipleship, the rapture, the resurrection, sin, judgment, communion, heaven, hell, eternal security and other doctrinal aspects.

Eschatology...The study of God. His revelation to, and relationship with, man.

Spiritual Gifts...The operation and experiences of divine gifting in the life of the believer.

Thanksgiving…The giving of thanks for blessings and help from the Lord. It is a thankful recognition of His awesome power in the life of the believer.

Miscellaneous…This type is for other not so well know or used types like Rapp etc.

As you can see, there are many types of poems and even more categories. I have tried to identify and elaborate on the major ones so you will have an idea of the scope and depth of the "Christian Poetic Expression". It's as big as ever and seems to keep expanding as we search out the truths of God.

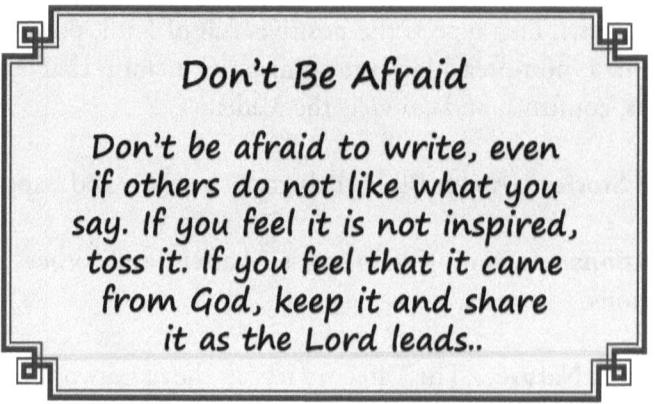

With Eagle Wings

I mounted up with eagle wings,
To soar above the clouds.
I viewed life above its trials,
Separate from the crowds.

Just me and God,
Together in the day.
With eagle wings,
He led the way.

Forgiveness and peace in a distance,
Suddenly I could see.
Joy and happiness trailed behind.
Then overshadowed me.

With eagle wings, I soared
Above life's every trial.
Now I walk by word of faith,
Rejoicing with every mile.

CHAPTER FOUR

Profile of a Christian Poet

I hear people saying, " I am not sure about my writing", "It isn't good enough", "I am not really a poet", "I just dabble at it", or what's worse, "I didn't have anything to do with it... it was all God"

Most of us feel that we are not really important in the process of creative writing. God does it all and we just hold the pen for Him to think and express Himself. This notion is very wrong. It goes against the Biblical teaching that says....We are co-laborers together with Christ and carry His anointing as a partner with the Holy Spirit in the ministry of reconciliation.

We need to get away from the idea that we are sub-standard and unworthy. After all, God created us in His own image. He wants us to express ourselves, but not in a fleshly show of self-ego, but rather as a demonstration of the inner spiritual person that we really are in Him. It is to this end that I attempt to profile a Christian poet.

The Christian poet should be:

1. **Confident:** That the Holy Spirit will be there to inspire the thought process.
2. **Courageous**: To pen the hearts cry, no matter if it's politically correct or not.

3. **Cautious**: To review, re-write, and edit until clarity and truth are obtained.
4. **Curious**: To inquire of God for a deeper revelation of life and experience.
5. **Caring**: Enough not to hurt the wounded soul, but rather to bless it.
6. **Commanding**: In authority over the stewardship of God's gifting.
7. **Courteous**: In the demonstration of the gift and presentation of its message.
8. **Concise**: In focus of thought and expression, without rambling.
9. **Concerned**: About anyone or everything that would hinder the flow of inspiration.
10. **Captured**: By God's love and holiness.
11. **Colorful**: In the use of modifiers, imagery and poetic expressions.
12. **Crazy**: Enough to follow after God and to stir up the gifting inside.
13. **Candid**: About life, personal experiences and one's deepest dreams.
14. **Crowned**: With the glory and beauty of the Lord.
15. **Creative**: In the development and construction of thoughts.
16. **Coordinated**: Enough to think and write at the same time.
17. **Covered:** With the wonderful anointing of His love.
18. **Crowded:** By rhymes of prayer and praise.
19. **Confined:** To biblical truth and the Christian life experience.
20. **Consumed:** By Divine revelation and visions of destiny.

The 20 C's listed above pretty well describe a Christian poet.

What does it say about you? Are you an, "I'm not sure," type of poet…who is afraid to stand up and be counted? I hope not. My prayer for you is that you stop caring about what others think and get to the business of enjoying your gifting as a Christian poet.

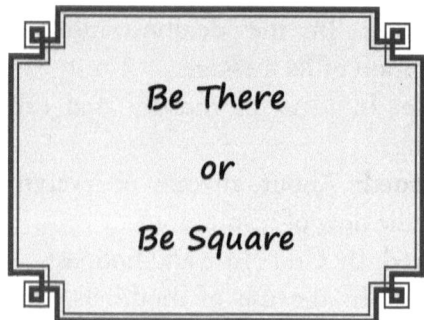

Poet of the Lord

Hear, Oh Poet of the Lord.
I offer you a great reward,
A gifting that shall never cease,
An outpouring of joy and peace.

I send you from my throne above,
As a messenger of my eternal love,
To a lost and dying land,
To every creature, every man.

Speak, Oh poet of the living God.
Dare to walk where angels trod.
Tell your world in rhymes of praise,
Of Jesus, whom from the dead I raised.

I give you words full of life.
Use them as an end to strife.
Send them by land and sea,
For this is your destiny.

I have chosen you especially by name,
So set aside your sorrow and shame,
And speak now on my behalf,
Of love and peace and even wrath.

Listen closely for my inner voice,
And pen your rhymes of choice.
Then cry aloud, as I speak to you,
So others may know me, as you do.

CHAPTER FIVE

RECOGNITION, SELF-WORTH AND POETRY

We all desire recognition and praise from our family, friends and the people around us. We'll even accept it from strangers.

We are creatures that need approval in order to go on in life. As a Christian, we are to draw that recognition from God and one another.

Here are excerpts from an e-mail that came to me that is typical of most of us.

> "Dear Bro. John:
>
> I want to take just a moment to thank you for the encouragement I have received from the Fellowship of Christian Poets. You will never know how God has used you to be such a blessing to my life. I am confident that God directed me to you. Though I had written some poetry, I had never defined myself as a poet until I became a member of the Fellowship of Christian Poets.
>
> Receiving the first recognition for my Thanksgiving poem in 2000 flipped a switch that turned on the inspiration to allow God to write through me. Then this year's honor bestowed as "Poet of the Year" has opened doors that I never dreamed.

Again, thank you for allowing me the privilege of representing FOCP as "Poet of the Year". May God continue to bless you with all the dreams and aspirations you have for FOCP for the future."

Linda Stevenson, Roanoke, VA

Linda is only one of many who are awed at the presence of God in their gifting and how He uses others as a source of blessings and assurance. She is also typical of most of us, who never really see ourselves as serious poets. After all, we are housewives, clerks, secretaries, salesmen, and lots of other ordinary folk with regular jobs.

Isn't it supposed to be the renown or famous that do great things? It can't be little old me that changes the world or makes a difference in the life of someone else. It is this lack of self-worth and insecurity that causes us to doubt and fall prey to the work of the devil, who seeks to extinguish the light of God's glory that dwells in us and shines through our gifting.

I am so very glad that Linda has come into that special awareness that God really does want to use her gifting to bless others and that she is indeed an instrument in His hands.

What about you? **Are you still feeling inadequate as a poet?** Are you questioning the seriousness of your calling? Do you say within yourself, "It's not a calling, just a hobby?".

Linda said, in her e-mail, that there was a point of recognition that turned on a light inside of her that let her know this thing was really of God. I think there are several things that turn on that mysterious inner light. Recognition is one, but there are others; things like faith, obedience, hope and sheer determination.

There's no getting around it, to be recognized is the best. When a fellowship or other group sees your talent and praises you for it, it's really great.

But what happens when you are not seen or praised? Most of us fall into that "Poor Me" void and either stop trying altogether or keep it to ourselves.

I still remember the hurts and the disappointments that fell upon me over the past 30 years, when my family said, **"I think you can do better"**. You know, I still get that. However, now I do not fall apart or get angry. I see it as a prompt from God… **"To Do Better."**

The devil will try and try to cut you up in little pieces with the well-meaning negative comments of family and friends. He will even bring criticism from so-called "authorities in the field".

It's up to you to recognize your calling, practice it often, and above all, take the negative as a prompt to strive for excellence.

It should be noted here that we should also watch out for the **"Chronic Critics"** who finds fault, just because. When you are pleased with your work and know that it is good, do not let the chronic critic steal your joy. Just consider the source and go on with what you are doing.

I must say that if we never received a positive comment, we should still follow our vision, because it was placed into our hearts by God and is ever-growing and will continue, until the hour of birth; when the world will stand up and take notice of what God has done. He is our comforter.

Some Christian poets do not realize the uniqueness and value of their gift. It comes on some of us suddenly and without warning and drives us through a thought process that leads to a whole new perspective. Most of us don't even know why. But I know why and therefore, I must tell you about this very special gifting. Consider it a gift for bewildered poets.

Your poetic flair is more than a passing fancy. It is a direct line to the heart of God. It's a channel that flows in the name of Jesus and is empowered by the Holy Spirit. You have been chosen ... to know the true and living God and also to reveal Him to those who are hurting, confused, lost, sick, lonely, heartbroken, depressed, and otherwise in need of Gods' love. You are a key player in God's master plan.

Your calling is Divine and everlasting. You cannot get away from it, even if you tried. You wake up in the middle of the night in a flow of poetic thought. You hear His voice at noonday and in the early morning hours.

God has given us a "Special Gifting". That is not to say that God favors us over others, but rather to say...we are given to know the mood of the Holy Spirit and the burden of His heart, for the purpose of poetic expression. That makes us unique and privileged, not better than. In fact, it creates even more of a responsibility, because we are called to communicate in a "heart to heart" expressive manor that by-passes the thought process and pierces the soul of those who read our poetry.

We have a "Special Anointing": There are many anointings. Some for healing, some for prophecy, teaching, evangelism, helps and so on. The poets' anointing is one of exhortation.

To exhort, according to Webster, is to urge, advise or caution, earnestly. That covers most of the gambit related to being an encourager...and that's what we really are.... one who urges, advises, and cautions.

We have been given a "Special Message": What we communicate in our poetry is all-important. Our message is the age-old story spoken in a new and living way. It's the expression of poetry that makes the old new again and more exciting than ever.

Those who have turned off religion are still open to the truth and it's your poetic voice that carries it past the dogma, the ritual and the prejudice.

I would like to illustrate the feeling and depth of our gift through the Christmas story, so you can see the application of God's gifting. But first, let's review the facts:

1. The birth of Jesus, the "Anointed One", was a turning point in history, for it was the incarnation of God in human flesh and that was an event of great magnitude. He who was promised by God finally came, after so many thousands of years, yet it was in the fullness of time that God sent His Only Son.

2. We know that His name was and still is called Jesus and that He is the Christ or "Anointed One".

3. We know that He was given so we could believe on Him and have eternal life (John 3:16),

4. We know that He was born to die for the sins of the whole world.

5. We know that He was resurrected from the dead and is now seated at the right hand of God, as King of kings and Lord of lords.

Wise Men Still Seek Him

Wise men still seek Him
Who appeared so long ago.
They come now by grace
Through faithful hearts aglow.

Wise men still seek Him,
For He is their "Bread of Life"
A sustaining inner strength
In times of sorrow or strife.

Wise men still seek Him,
The Christ of Calvary.
God's only begotten Son
Crucified as sin's penalty.

Wise men still seek Him
Jesus, God in human array.
King of kings and Lord of lords
Born to earth on Christmas day.

All of this knowledge and more, we joyfully celebrate during the Christmas holiday season. However, our poetry is more heart-felt and more deeply expressed because of that "Special Gifting", because of that "Special Anointing", and because that "Special Message" dwells deep within our hearts. It is the foundation of our faith. It's a very special gift from our Heavenly Father and what makes our gifting of poetry so exciting.

Let me encourage you to develop your gift and use your talent for the glory of the Lord. He has already recognized you. In His sight, you are accepted. When we realize, as Linda Stevenson did, that God is happy with us and wants us to be a channel through which others can benefit, we will settle down and begin the real work of being used by God.

"I AM" There

"I AM" There,
At the end of your broken dreams,
Before the Sun rises over your day,
Prior to those tear-filled streams.

"I AM" There,
Down that road of despair,
When all seems to be lost,
And no one wants to care.

"I AM" There,
Over all of life's twists and turns,
When tomorrow is all but gone,
And when you are full of concerns.

"I AM" There,
Sayeth the Lord of Host,
To bring you hope and peace,
And the power of my Holy Ghost.

"I AM" There,
To be sure you make it through,
In the midst of every trial,
To bless your life and deliver you.

"I Am" There

CHAPTER SIX

POETRY, THE LANGUAGE OF LOVE

Poetry is for lovers ... and who best to express love than the greatest lover of all. Who is the greatest lover of all? Is it perhaps you or possibly me?

Who, pray tell, is the greatest lover of all?

It's not Casanova, nor is it one of us. It is none other than God, your Heavenly Father, which is characterized in the scriptures in a short but to the point statement...***God is Love***.... He is the greatest lover of all.

He so loved the world, (that's you and me), that he gave His only Son, (that's Jesus, the Christ), to be sacrificed on a cruel cross, as a penalty for sin. This is true love, to lay down your life for another.

There is no greater love than this, for it is the ultimate expression of love. That's what draws us to God, His everlasting unselfish and endless love. He really cares about us and is always seeking new ways to bless us.

What does poetry have to do with love? Why, it is the language of love. See it in your spirit's eye by reading the Song of Solomon. Listen to it as the Holy Spirit speaks to you in that quiet; almost still voice, in words of encouragement, faith and hope.

Now this is a test … When, if ever, have you spoken in poetry, to your Heavenly Father? Has there ever been a procession of poetic thought that is filled with love for Him? He speaks to us all the time and it is always in words filled with love.

I can remember the 1st year of my marriage. I must have written my wife, Marilyn over 300 love poems. We are now approaching our 39th year. The written poems have given way to the verbal expression. However, I tell her of my love more than once every day and support that verbal flair with multiple acts of encouragement.

I do this because I love her and I have learned about love from God, my Heavenly Father. He teaches me to love and shows me how to act…See Galatians Chapter five for the fruit of the Spirit, a list of how love is to be expressed towards your lover.

I must admit that I haven't written 300 love poems to Jesus. But I have on many occasions expressed my love for God in poetry. Here's one that I particularly like:

Fragile Flower Red

As a flower in earthen sod,
I bloom for thee, oh God.
To blossom with the turn of spring;
To be to you, a beautiful thing.

I lift my Fragile Flower Red
Upward from my earthen bed,
To draw light from God above,
Strength and peace and joy and love.

As a flower, I bloom for thee,
That passersby may stop and see.
Your fragrance and beauty I am,
Flowered in grace, as a man.

As a flower in earthen sod,
I bloom for thee, oh God.
Upward, I lift my head,
As a Fragile Flower Red.

My heart cries out for the living God and my life to be filled with His glory. The psalmists said it well, "Who is man, that God should pay any attention to him?" Yet He does pay attention and is deeply concerned about our well-being. I guess that's why Jesus said, "I'll never leave you or forsake you" and that He will be with us, even to the end of the age.

What manner of man is this? What great and magnificent love is this? That would allow a "Fragile Flower Red", such as I, to bloom for Him and to express His great love in the earth. Who would ever think that God would allow man to live and to have being in Him?

Doesn't that just knock your socks off?

If you are living outside of the blessings (love) of God and find yourself in sadness and gloom, may I suggest that you go back to the Word of God, which contains His love letters to you and discover His love all over again. It's all there in black and white with red letters, if you have that edition. Then sit down and speak to God. Let your gifting flow in poetic words of praise, adoration and love. Use His language of love to tell Him how much you love and appreciate Him.

We, as Christian poets, should be having a love affair with God. He so desires to love us and be loved by us. It's the best thing that could ever happen to us. God really wants a deep abiding fellowship with His children.

The Lord said through Jeremiah, the prophet, " But let him that seeks glory, glory in this: That he understands and knows me, that I am the Lord, which exercises loving kindness, judgment, and righteousness in the earth: For in these things I delight, " sayeth the Lord.

His love is kind. His judgment is full of mercy, and His righteousness is full of light. They empower us with words of love that can be spoken and written for the benefit of others. They create a sense of well-being, security and hope inside us. They keep us from the destruction that comes from fear, rejection, persecution, and a host of other adversities.

Poetry, in the normal world, takes all kinds of shapes, sizes, techniques, and displays many unusual faces. However, in the world of Christian poetry, there is only one face. It's the face of Love.

The "Christian Poetic Expression" is a portrait of a unique and dynamic relationship with our Lord Jesus. He is our inspiration, our reason to share, our drive to sit down with a pen or at a computer to express ourselves. This is our destiny…to share God's love. What better way than through the very gift given to us through the Holy Spirit…the gifting of poetry.

The love of God through poetry does four things:

1. It breaks down the self-defense barriers set up around the reader and penetrates the heart, planting the glorious Word of God that is often wrapped in a cloak of poetry.
2. It blesses, encourages, provokes, and even heals the reader's broken heart.
3. It instructs, challenges, and strengthens with emotional stability.
4. It leads, guides, and calls to the reader for his or her time and attention.

Question! Which of these are you currently doing? What, if anything, are you doing to share God's love through your poems? Who has benefited from your poetic gift? How you answer these questions will show your level of commitment to your gift and obedience to your calling as a Christian poet.

Poetry is the language of love. Let's use it more often to express ourselves.

CHAPTER SEVEN

DIVINE INSPIRATION

To be inspired by God is a good thing. It is the source of all Christian Poetry. However, inspiration means different things to different folks.

Some poets claim inspiration as though it was a mystical power, outside of themselves. They take no credit for the composition and formatting of their work, saying" It was given of God, not me"

There are other poets that labor over their poetic expressions to be sure it makes sense before sharing it with others. Their inspiration, so they say, comes in bits and pieces that have to be clarified, modified, and properly arranged.

Who is right? What is inspiration anyway? Many poems are inspired but not anointed.

Anointing versus Inspiration

Inspiration, according to Webster is: "an inspiring or animating action or influence." When something is inspired, like a thought or idea, it carries one or all of Webster's definition for "Animating or Animate" which are:

1. to give life to.
2. to give zest to.
3. to move or stir to action.

The source of this inspiration can be almost anything or anyone. It could be the beauty of the morning sky; the words of a co-worker; a T. V. show. It can also be the Holy Spirit. However, if God inspires it, He also anoints it.

The difference between anointing and inspiration is this; Webster again says to anoint is: 1. to apply oil to. 2. to consecrate by applying oil. The notion is to smear or rub all over until it soaks into the skin and gets into the blood stream.

When applied to the spiritual, it means that the Holy Spirit is smearing or rubbing His presence upon whatever or whomever He chooses to anoint, thus creating a reflection of God in the earth. If that is you, then you carry His presence with you and carry His thoughts within your being and become His reflection. If it is your poem, the same applies.

Inspiration, on the other hand, does not carry the thoughts of God or His presence unless He has also anointed it. The beauty of a morning sky has no power to anoint. But you, as a human being, have the intellect and ability to draw from it, using your own creativity, to fashion a poem, create an new thought, or even a product for resale. This type of inspiration is used in many marketing campaigns.

So how do you know if your poem is anointed? Ask yourself this one question; do you sense a Divine presence in the message, in the words, and in the thought process? If so, you know that the Holy Spirit is there, laboring with you to complete the work. Does this notion sound strange? Didn't Jesus say, "Lo I'll be with you always?" He is with us through the Holy Spirit.

Our inspiration comes from the Holy Spirit who sometimes guides us by influencing our thoughts but leaves the details up to us as to form and exact wording. At other times, the Holy Spirit will take control, putting the exact words into out thought process thereby influencing the output of our content.

Most of us have poems that fit both the guiding and controlling aspects of Divine Inspiration. However, it is my feeling that whether a poem is completely of God or a co-laboring effort, it will still meet certain basic guidelines that distinguish it as a good poem.

There are lots of ways to critique a poem. These five make more sense to me than any others. They are:

1. Balanced rhyme and meter
2. A central thought or expression
3. Understandable language
4. An acceptable length
5. A redeeming value or quality.

However, to say that your poem is straight from heaven, without your participation, is incorrect. Why, because it is born out of fellowship and fellowship is a meeting of the minds and the joining of the hearts. It is all of God…and all of you, fashioned as a symphony of thought that is filled with truth and spiritual expression.

Sometimes the, "all of you" requires editing to refine its clarity and smooth its understanding. Sometimes the, "all of God" comes to us as a fleeting thought or a revelation of truth that takes revision and editing as we seek to put it down on paper so others can understand its meaning.

As we commune with the Father in prayer and discuss our inner feelings with Jesus, the Holy Spirit begins to speak to our hearts. His gentle presence is felt as He begins to open up the floodgates of God's Divine love.

Before you know it, you are fashioning a rhyme or jotting down a thought that has suddenly dropped into your spirit. Your prayers of thanksgiving and the words of praise that filled your heart are suddenly spilling over onto the pages of a note pad. God has come alive and you are in the middle of a full- fledged triune relationship.

Out of this triune fellowship comes the "Christian Poetic Expression". It looks much like love and feels almost like joy and tastes a lot like peace. It is an ever emerging and beckoning call that drives you to return to that place of intimacy, again and again. It is here that we perceive and come to understand and write about.

Our joy, as Christian poets, is to know this great fellowship and share it with the world. We, the poets of God, so speak that the people of earth may hear and understand the greatness of our God and His overwhelming love.

Every Christian has a built-in gateway that regulates the flow of Inspiration. For some, it's a quiet awareness; for others, it's an unusual sensory perception; for most, it is an indescribable feeling that, "you know that you know."

The Christian poet is no different than other Christians. This quiet awareness, this unusual perception, or a "knowing that you know" feeling must be attained before inspiration flows. However, there is also a Divine calling that fosters authorship and mandates expression.

This "Divine Calling" is an invitation to pen the flow of inspirational thought. The Spirit beckons us. We are shown, yet allowed to see for ourselves.

We scurry to pen what we hear and see in the Spirit. We strive for proper verse arrangement, and pray that what we write is actually born of the Spirit. Something inside of us tells us when the transfer is complete and when the verses are properly arranged.

We **"know that we know."** This is our "Built-in Gateway" It's that quiet assurance or that unusual perception that tells us that we were in His presence and able to understand His thoughts. Our joy is to fashion them in a coherent word array that will bless all who read its message.

There are several specific conditions to discovering your own gateway. They are:

1. You must be "Born Again".
2. You must be filled with the Spirit.
3. You must accept your calling as a co-author of Divine thought.
4. You must be obedient to the call accept the invitation to write.
5. You must spend time with the Holy Spirit who is the keeper of gateway.

If you are struggling with your compositions and never quite feel the sense of completion, it could be because you have never entered through the "Built-in Gateway" given to every true believer.

Search your heart, pray and seek the Lord for that "know that you know", quiet awareness that all is well. He wants you to rest in His love and know that you are in His will.

Let us look towards the Holy Spirit for Divine guidance and/or control as we pen the words that bless those around us. But do not be afraid to use your editing pen to fashion a work of art that reflects you, as well as, the one who inspires you.

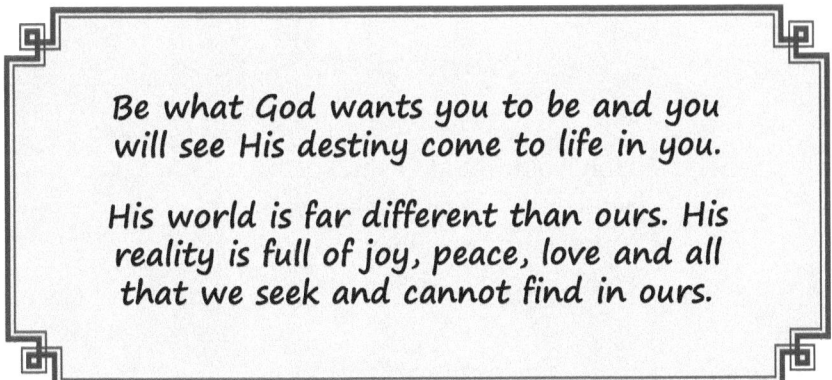

Be what God wants you to be and you will see His destiny come to life in you.

His world is far different than ours. His reality is full of joy, peace, love and all that we seek and cannot find in ours.

Holy Spirit

Holy Spirit, Lord Divine
Send your love and make it mine.
Come Lord Jesus, for all to see.
Holy Spirit, breathe on me.

Holy Spirit, Lord Divine
Fill my heart with new wine.
Come Lord Jesus, hear my plea.
Holy Spirit, breathe on me.

Holy Spirit, Lord Divine
Be my Lord, all the time.
Come Lord Jesus,
My life to Thee.

Holy Spirit, breathe on me.
Lord of Glory, I come to Thee.
Holy Spirit, breathe on me.
Come, Lord Jesus, Come for me.

CHAPTER EIGHT

POETRY AND HOLY SPIRIT CONVICTION

There is something about poetry that causes us to evaluate ourselves when we write it or when we read it. It must be the power of the Holy Spirit, as He invites us to fashion a poem and think about what we are saying. This is seen more than ever in the attempt to write around a particular theme, like the "Good Samaritan." I have read many different approaches related to this theme.

As I attempt my own words, I cannot help but reflect on the true meaning of the parable and if I have lived up to what Jesus said, **"Go and do likewise."**

Am I like the Priest or the Levite? Do I turn my head and pass by those in need? These questions and more flood my mind with the convicting power of the Holy Spirit as I write, review, edit and pray. What does it do for you?

Are you also under God's conviction, as you write, read, edit and share your gift?

Conviction is a strange thing. It is a kind of knowledge or expectation that you know and understand as God's perfect will, but some- times fall short of. It is the subject matter that you undertake to write about that brings all this about.

The subject matter, being a part of the Word of God, illuminates our souls and acts as a judge, comparing our imperfection to His perfection. This leaves us hanging in the balance. It's as though the Lord says to our spirit, **"Walk out what you talk."** If you write about a parable and truly understand its meaning, you also must live up to its light.

It's not easy to write a poem about a particular parable without restating what has already been said. To get the central truth across and bring the message home so the reader can understand and know what they should be doing, is a real challenge.

As I read my own poem, I realize that I need to be this generation's **"Good Samaritan."** It is our calling from God…to **"Go and do likewise"**. I have resolved to apply what I have re-learned by fashioning a poem and to, with eyes wide open, will look for the opportunity to be a neighbor to someone in need.

The Good Samaritan

(Luke 10:30-37)

Jesus exampled a Samaritan,
To illustrate, "who is our neighbor."
He spoke of a man in His day,
That was not in religious favor.

The "Good Samaritan" helped,
When a certain man fell among thieves.
While others just passed on by,
He stopped to tend to his needs.

Our world, like the "Good Samaritan's,
Is filled with those in need.
The fatherless, the hungry, and so on,
Who wait for a "Good Samaritan" indeed.

Jesus said that we should do likewise,
 As the "Good Samaritan" in his day.
To stretch forth a helping hand,
To all who have fallen along life's way.

CHAPTER NINE

POETRY IN MOTION

We should always be looking to put our poetry in motion. It begins by Divine revelation and/or as a demand against our gifting. Usually we will see a therapeutic style that helps others but first ministers to us. The motion of poetry is seen best in the oral presentation as a performance.

Origin = Revelation

Divine revelation is a term used a lot in Christian circles today. Both the charismatic believer and the fundamentalist claim a direct link to God. Both openly reveal their relation- ship with the Lord in terms like, "the Lord told me" or "God spoke to me." This is indeed a mystery to those who do not know the Lord. They often laugh saying, "God talks to you?", as if we were crazy. But we know, nevertheless, that God has revealed Himself to us in ways that are un-mistakably real.

Poetic revelation has five distinct characteristics:

1. It is a direct communication with the Lord.
2. It is always in line with the Bible.
3. It is mostly personal in nature.
4. It is rooted in love, even when corrective.
5. It is verifiable through other witnesses.

Poetic revelation is not the "end-all" to one's dilemma. It is the sharing of a brief moment inside the heart of God. It's when His feelings touch yours in a oneness that causes you to see as He sees and feel as He feels. Instead of a word from the Lord that helps you to make it through, Its a viewpoint, a happening, an encounter, an unspoken feeling that can only be expressed by the poetic gifting given to you, the poet.

Some would say that this is nothing more than seeing in the Spirit, which many Old Testament prophets experienced. This is true. Poets often see in the Spirit, however, those same Old Testament prophets flowed with poetic verse. In fact, much of the Old Testament was written in poetic verse.

When was the last time you had a "Poetic Revelation"? I can remember one time in the recent past when God opened His heart to me. The language flowed like running water but the message was one of awe and holiness.

As you read the following poem, you will quickly see that this was a happening that God wanted me to see. I still get goose bumps when I read this poem, because I had the distinct feeling, when I was writing it, that it was and even now is happening in heaven.

The Angels Cry Holy

The angels cry "Holy,"
While sorrow fills the land.
For God's Judgment Day,
Is to come upon every man.

The angels cry "Holy,"
While mankind goes astray,
Rejecting the love of God,
To follow his own precarious way.

The angels cry "Holy,"
Knowing the terror of the Lord,
When all who dwell in sin,
Will suddenly be destroyed.

The angels cry "Holy,"
Waiting for all things new,
Born of the Holy Spirit,
When God's Judgment is through.

The angels cry "Holy,"
"Holy is the Lamb,"
Waiting for the children of God,
To join the great "I AM"

Method = By Design
The "Stirring Up" Process

Consider this: Paul recognized a gift in Timothy and told him that he should "Stir Up" the gift that God had given him. In other words, he was to practice the gift, control it and be sure it is regularly operating in and through him.

The same is true for any gift including poetry. The principle is applicable to all that possess gifts from the Holy Spirit. Quite often we will need to "Stir Up" the gift to keep it alive in us. This is poetry by design.

Poetry by design is different than the **"God Gave It To Me"** poetry. It is where the poet carefully selects the topic, style, and even other elements of the design before fashioning the verse. It is a deliberate act of selection without waiting for the move of the Spirit.

Poetry by design requires a careful review of the finished product. There will be many editing sessions in a line-by-line evaluation:

"Is it theologically sound?"
"Is it uplifting?"
"Is it easy to read and understand?"
"Is the meter correct?"
"Is it centered around a Biblical Truth?"

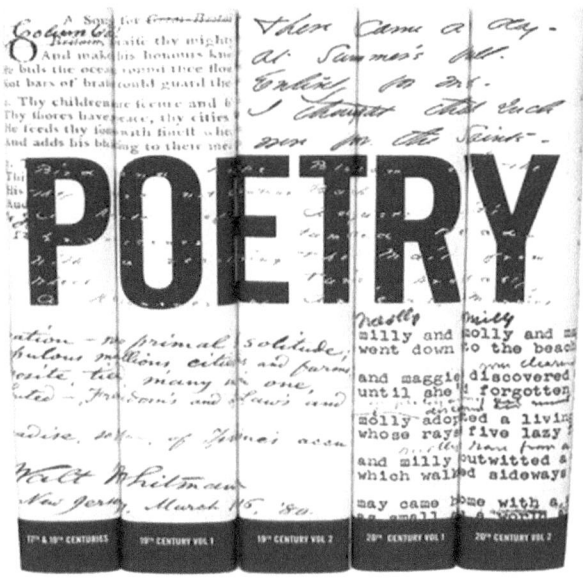

All of these questions and more will come into play as the poet prepares the text and works through the design process. They are all contributing factors that "Stir Up" the gift and link the poet to God's inspiration.

The poet must have confidence in the gift. That is to say, he or she must rest in the fact that God is not an "Indian Giver". The gifts and calling of God are without repentance…That is to say; God does not repent or regret that He gave you the gift in the first place.

This confidence puts a demand on God to cause the gift to operate at our command. It's as if God has said, "Here's a special gift. Now go ahead and use it as often as you want to."

The Demand For Inspiration

This demand upon God for inspiration is no different than what we read in the New Testament. Consider these…"You have not because you ask not", "Seek and ye shall find", "Knock and the door shall be opened unto you",

All of these scriptures put the responsibility on the believer to call upon God, or to place a demand upon God for something that He has already made available.

If you seek, you will find. If you knock, the door gets opened. If you don't ask, you do not receive. In every case there is a, "You That Must Do". It's no different with the gift of poetry. We must place a demand upon God to inspire us when we need it, when we want it, when we feel the time is right.

To "Stir Up" then is to put a demand upon the Lord to cause the gift inside us to operate at our command so we can exercise it at will.

The Nature and Scope of "Poetry by Design"

Poetry by design is topical in nature. It envelops the entire Christian doctrine, from "Heaven to Hell", from "Christmas to Easter" and back again. It focuses on Biblical truth and personal experience.

I set out to compose a poetic story that would reveal a biblical truth. I expected the gift that God gave me to operate and I began to write, without knowing where I would end up.

The gift operated. The Holy Spirit joined me in the process, and I fashioned a few good stories that have blessed many through the years. Try it some time. It's a challenge and lots of fun.

The Single Most Effective Tool

Faith is the single most effective tool available to the poet. This faith is no more than simple confidence in the Lord, who is the Master of all gifts. There can be no, "I can't do it". There must be, "I can do all things through Christ who gives me strength".(Galatians 2:20)

Faith provides the substance from which the hopeful expression will be fashioned. It also provides the evidence that it will come into existence. Thus, the poem lies in the demand for inspiration and in the confidence that the Lord will continue to allow the gift to operate at your command. Faith seeks to find, knocks with anticipation, and speaks as though it was when it is not yet visible. It is your most effective tool in fashioning a rhyme by design.

The Skill-Benefit

Poetry by design causes the poet to become skilled at a craft that is ever emerging out of a gifting given by God. Instead of waiting for something to happen, the poet makes it happen by focusing attention on the task and putting a demand upon the Lord for inspiration.

Thus, the novice grows into a skilled poet who fashions biblical truths in a topical array of subject matter that blesses all who read.

Poetry by design is the growth process that transforms a would-be poet into an accomplished artist who is fully equipped for the master's use.

May the Lord bless you with sudden inspiration that flows from Divine revelation and with the confidence to utilize the gifting within you at anytime.

Agreeing With God

> I'll speak of things that are not,
> Believing in them as though they were.
> Because my Heavenly Father spoke them first,
> In glorious promises that never ever blur.
>
> I'll take Him at His word,
> And listen to all He has to say.
> I'll wrap each promise around my soul,
> Until what was spoken becomes my day.
>
> I will agree with my Lord,
> Trusting that He knows best.
> For only His awesome power,
> Can provide my soul with rest.

Style = Therapeutic

Poetry can be therapeutic, meaning that, it can help you get through a difficult situation. Much of the Hebrew poetry found in the Psalms is therapeutic. They begin with a cry to God for help, and then shift to a repetitive proclamation of faith.

"Therapeutic" means ... to serve a cure, heal, or maintain health.
(Webster's Dictionary, College Edition)

If you are writing Christian poems that are mostly sad or full of tears to God with only the last few lines reflecting faith and hope, you're not writing therapeutic poetry. You are writing "Negative" poetry that is sure to relate to depressed readers, keeping them depressed.

Negative poetry is much like country music. It focuses on sadness that captures the reader's emotions. It presents a scenario that causes the reader to dwell on his or her own hurts, which may or may not be similar. This is the "Empathy Road" to depression and continual torment. It's the devil's way of spreading "Doom and Gloom".

"Sorrow is my morning drink.
I am lost, confused and alone.
Where are you dear God?
That I may find my way home."

This is the beginning of a poem that can inspire or depress. It can develop negatively or stay positive. The balance between the negative and positive flow will determine its therapeutic value.

If I continue with a saddened, poor me tone, I will most likely appeal to inner feelings, which are similar to yours, causing you to dwell on them again. You may even applaud my poem as being good, because you related to it so well. And since misery loves company, our journey together will take a downward spiral into sadness instead of an upward leap of faith.

On the other hand, I can state the negative, like the psalmist of old, but keep the poem positive by making statements of faith that foster hope and trust in God, which will keep you from sadness and lead you into the joy of the Lord. Too much emphasis in the negative will kill any hope of real encouragement or other ministerial possibilities.

The above stanza knocks at the reader's heart and encourages active participation. They might say within themselves, "That's the way I feel?" or" emotionally, they might conclude, "You've got my attention...now what?"

"I will wait upon the Lord,
And hope in His mercy.
He will not hide His love,
Or reject my earnest plea."

These two statements of faith bring hope to others and encourage them to also turn unto the Lord, who is their only real help in times of despair. I could have continued in the negative, taking them deeper into a pit of hopelessness, but that would not be "Therapeutic" because it would not heal the broken heart, or set the captive free.

Therapeutic poetry maintains good health. It does not destroy it. If you hear a poem that makes you cry and leaves you with a saddened spirit, it is not therapeutic. It is most likely an outgrowth from the "flesh" crying out for attention and solace for a bruised ego.

The fact that you have been saddened by someone else's poem proves the point that the poem was not therapeutic. It did not maintain good emotional health in you. Instead, it led you to a place of vulnerability where the enemy can easily defeat you.

If you are using poetry as a therapy for yourself or a friend, try nipping the negative flow early on and begin making positive statements of faith. You'll quickly discover that your own depression will begin to lift and you will begin to see the light at the end of the tunnel.

Many of the psalms are therapeutic, meaning they are cries
to God in times of despair. However, the Hebrew poets never stayed in the valley of depression for very long. Their writings contain an acknowledgement of the problem; their cry to God and their

confession of faith is for the loving kindness and power of God to deliver them. It was never a soul-searching pity party.

Writing secular poems about your vices or doom and gloom experiences helps no one, not even you. It only causes the reader to identify with their hurt that might be similar and opens the door for them to go back and suffer some more. This is not God's way of redemption. He calls us to repentance and faith in Jesus and leads us into a new day and a new abundant life. He leads us to an overcomer status and takes away our victim mentality. It's okay to capture your deepest feelings in poetic form, even if they are depressing. Over the years, your poetry will paint a vivid picture of your Spiritual growth. However, you should realize that, if you share them with others, you could bring a cloud of gloom to those who may be hurting inside like you were when you penned the verses.

Most readers will reject any poem that stays too long in the negative and keeps them captured in empathy, sorrow, or feelings.

God bless you as you understand and compose "Therapeutic" poetry.

From Tears To Smiles

They attack from every side.
Zing!! Go their arrows of pride.
Like demons up from the pit of hell,
They come to laugh at those who fell.

They care not how hard you've tried.
They're here to kill God's love inside.
But though insults come our way,
We'll still find peace most every day.

> God is greater than all their dares.
> The Holy Spirit proves He cares.
> When we're faced with many trials,
> God will replace our tears with smiles.

Delivery = Performance

The Christian poet's goal is to put **"Poetry In Motion" through "Love And Devotion"**. There are lots of ways to do this, dance, drama, and music, just to name a few. When poetry is put in motion, it becomes a performance. The type of performance depends upon us.

One of the best examples today of "Performance Poetry" is Rapp. You may not like all the lyrics but the style, presentation and mood are all performance. Rapp accentuates the meter while stressing the message in a predictable rhyme sequence.

Carmen has perfected this style for the Christian audience by slowing down the tempo and using meaningful words and expressions to communicate the good news of Jesus Christ. His exclusive use of poetic verse makes his style a work of art and one of the best examples of "Performance Poetry"

Another example of performance and presentation is the Monologue: a solo presentation of an event or action before an audience. This requires total concentration and lots of memory skills. It is you, all alone in front of everyone, with all eyes on you.

A third example of "Performance Poetry" is the story poem. Imagine a semicircle of three to five-year-olds seated around a "Storyteller." It might be a book or an imaginary story told to the children during a time of learning. The children are waiting with excitement as the "Storyteller" spins the yarn before the group. It might go something like this:

A story for you...and a story for me...
This is the story of a little chicken
Who once sat on my knee

The children wait to hear what will happen next to that chicken, while the "Storyteller" continues. Their minds are active with imagination as the "Storyteller" performs the story in a simple oral interpretation.

We all enjoy listening to someone who can share a dream and capture our interest. Poets are or should be "Storytellers". They should perform their work as an actor plays out a particular role.

Performance Poetry has seven basic elements that are unmistakable. They are:

1. The use of word pictures that engage the imagination.
2. The application of rhyme and meter in every verse.
3. The conveyance of body language during the presentation.
4. Strong emotion to accentuate speech patterns.
5. A variance in tone to denote changes in character or action.
6. A memorized pathway from beginning to end.
7. The use of gestures and hand movements to involve the audience.

To perform a poem is to bring it to life in an array of emotion and body language that captures the attention of those who listen. It is both visual and verbal which is the most powerful means of communication.

Now think about the last time you stood up to read a poem. Was it an experience that stirred the audience? Did it capture their imagination? Were you trembling with a quivering voice or were you confidant, assured, and persuasive? You do not have to be an actor to perform your poetry.

A good oral presentation can be made by paying attention to the small things like good posture; reading the poem over several times before presenting it; looking for accent words to vary tone or volume; maintaining good eye contact with the audience and watching body movements to insure they do not detract from your presentation.

The most important element in "Performance Poetry" is memorization. If you have it memorized, you are free from the paper version and able to really experiment with style and delivery.

Let us dedicate ourselves to better presentations that will invoke God's power, anointing, and grace upon the lives of those who hear our poems.

God bless you as you "Perform" your poetry on the stages of life.

Speak With Authority

A Whisper in the Wind

There's a whisper in the wind,
That lingers both day and night.
A champion of truth and justice,
By the power of His might

A word in due season,
That echoes from deep within.
A voice out of nowhere,
Reproving the world of sin.

Look there, in the street,
And here, by the shores of the sea.
There's a whisper hidden in the wind,
A voice from eternity.

There's a calling from God.
His voice is hidden in the wind.
In a whisper, He speaks
With the counsel of a friend.

Listen for the "Whisper",
All who seek to know.
It is God's Holy Spirit,
Telling you which way to go.

CHAPTER TEN

BIBLICAL CONCEPTS AND POETRY

Biblical concepts are what make up the belief system we, as followers of Christ, take hold of, believe, and adhere to in our walk with God. These concepts are treasured, studied and interpreted to form theological foundations for our faith. They include such ideas as: "The Rapture" of the Church, "The 2nd Coming" of Christ, "The Resurrection" of the Dead, "The Blood Atonement", "Final Judgment", "Salvation" by Grace, "Hell", "Heaven", The "Sovereignty" of God, The "Free Will" of Man and so on.

I would like to examine the Biblical concept called, "The Atonement". This is what we celebrate every Easter, yet many major denominations have left off the idea that one should die for all...that Jesus was and always will be the blood sacrifice to God and atonement for our sins. How sad that they should ignore God's only way to cleanse us from our own sins. (I John 1:9)

The Old Testament sacrificial system, that demanded the pure lamb as a sacrifice for sin on the Day of Atonement, was an annual portrait of the cross.

Hundreds of years before it actually happened, the prophet Isaiah prophesized that the Messiah or Christ would pay sin's awful price.

(Chapter 53.) Jesus told the woman at the well that He was the Christ or "Anointed One" sent from God. He also told His disciples that He was to be crucified for the sins of the entire World.

The very concept of Christianity is centered on the cross and it's "Blood Atonement." To reject this is to deny God's only way of salvation. Those who do are "Anti-Christ's."

We, as Christian poets, write about the cross of Jesus, the reason for His death, and of His resurrection from the dead. We do this because we are compelled to testify of our faith and that we have been forgiven. We share our poetry any- where and everywhere we can to proclaim the "Good News" that Jesus died for us so we could live for Him.

You cannot discuss Christian poetry without talking about theology. They go hand in hand. However, I need to explain the meaning of theology. In its basic meaning it is, the science of the study of God. However, it also can be described as "Biblical Truth". Now read this poem and see if you can find the Biblical truths. As you seek to know, you will engage in the science of the study of God, known as "Theology".

A Gift From The God Of Eternity

They traveled by light of shining star
From lands both near and very far ...
To see what God had one,
To pay tribute to His only on.

Wise men and shepherds and angels too,
Made haste to see this "Big To Do".
Son of God made Son of Man ...
Born of a virgin in Bethlehem.

A little child in a far away land,
Known in eternity as the great "I AM".
Came to show us a more excellent way,
To live life in abundance every day.

Wrapped in simple swaddling clothes,
From holy head to tiny toes,
And placed in a manger's stall,
Though He is Lord of all.

The WORD of God in human flesh,
Given to all by Spirit's breath.
They called Him, "JESUS of Galilee"
A gift from the God of eternity.

Well, what did you discover? Here's what I see:

1. The light of a shining star led wise men and shepherds to the birthplace of Jesus.
2. It was deemed "Wise" to pay tribute (Honor) to God's only Son.
3. God sent His only Son to be born as a man.
4. Jesus pre-existed as God in Heaven prior to His birth and gave it all up to be born into the human experience. He was indeed God in human form.
5. Everyone made a big "To Do" over His birth, including the angels of Heaven.
6. He came to show us a more excellent way.
7. He is Lord of all even though He was born in a stall.
8. He was the Word described in John 1:1-12 who was made flesh.
9. His life is duplicated (Given) to us by the indwelling of the Holy Spirit.
10. His name is Jesus and He is our gift from eternity.

What does all this really mean? Jesus Himself made it very clear when He said, John 3:16, "For God so loved the world, that He gave His only Son, that whosoever believeth on Him should not perish, but have everlasting life."

Jesus was God incarnate. (God in human flesh) John 1:1-12 and Philippians, chapter two tell us this great truth. This means that no one could save us from our sin but God. He did just that, by sending us a Savior, who would live out the human experience, without sin and willingly pay the price for sin, (Death), that we could come to God through Him.

Christmas is our celebration of His denial of power from a Heavenly throne to a human dependency upon God and a human defeat of God's enemies including death itself. What better reason to give thanks to God and praise to Jesus that His willingness to enter our world to deliver us from our own shortfalls. This is the real meaning of Christmas and why we should celebrate His birth.

It has occurred to me that some poets might not know how to write a short Biblically based thematic poem. Therefore, I want to share some of my thoughts with you on the subject and encourage you to try.

The following poem is an example of one that has been placed in Holy Land USA Nature Park, in Bedford, VA. (There are 19 poems, everyone are on 3' by 4' Signs)

Types and Shadows

Types and shadows
Are all around.
In Abraham and Isaac,
They are surely found.

Isaac, a willing participant,
At the hands of his father's knife.
A test of love and obedience,
A shadow of salvation's light.

Obedient to his father,
Ready to offer up his soul.
Isaac, lay upon the altar,
So the Bible story is told.

Yet Isaac's life was spared,
As God provided another sacrifice.
He was only a "Type" and a "Shadow",
Of Jesus, who paid sin's awful price.

The story is obviously about Abraham getting ready to sacrifice his only son, Isaac. That location is depicted at Holy Land USA. My poem is thematic set to Isaac being a "Type" and a "Shadow" of Jesus.

The theme must be identified first before you write. Note that the theme is different than the story. As in many Bible stories, there can be several meanings or messages. I am sure you can see other truths, as well as, the one I chose. The theme here was selected before I began the poem. It gave me a direction so I wouldn't ramble on or stray off my purpose.

Next there is the story itself...the events need to be there of what happened but, do not need to be in Biblical verse. Sometimes, a general overview is enough. Just telling the story, however, is a waste of time because anyone can read it for himself or herself in the Bible.

You must add **Inspiration, Creativity and Interest** to capture the reader's attention. That means it must be thought provoking. I added these crucial elements by focusing on Isaac as the central character. I showed his willingness to be the sacrifice and his obedience to his father's will, all characteristics of Jesus.

Finally, there is the "Power Point" that brings home the central truth of the poem, which is also the theme. It tells why I wrote it in the first place. Usually it's a sum up or conclusion at the end. Here's mine:

Yet Isaac's life was spared, as God provided another sacrifice. He was only a type and a shadow, of Jesus, who paid sin's awful price.

Particular attention needs to be paid to the following:

1. Theme
2. Overall Story
3. Main Character
4. Central Truth
5. Power Point or Conclusion

We, as Christian poets, need to rightly divide the "Word of Truth" (Bible), in order to capture the splendor of its majesty. What you say is important.

Repetition is another way to drive home a biblical concept or thought. When applied to poetry, the repetition becomes the power point for the central thought of your expression. When you use repetition there are seven rules or guidelines to keep in mind. They are:

1. The repetition needs to be a clear and meaningful descriptive of the person or place where the action occurs.

2. One line of each quatrain should be repetitive of one of the lines in the 1st stanza.
3. The sum total of all quatrains (Stanzas) should support one central thought or theme.
4. Additional verbiage within each quatrain should amplify the action described in the repetition through word pictures, feelings, or analogies. This is the **WHO, WHAT, WHEN, WHERE, HOW and WHY** that form the details.
5. The length of the poem should not exceed five or at the most six quatrains to guard against rambling.
6. The title of the poem should be a purposeful emphasis of the repetition.
7. The poem should build upon the repetition to form an expository look at the central theme.

Here's a poem that describes what I mean in the seven rules above.

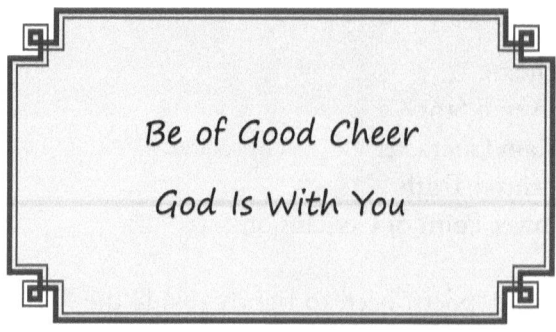

In A Twinkle of An Eye

In the winkle of an eye,
The Lord will come for me.
Before you can even blink,
I'll be with Jesus in eternity.

In the twinkle of an eye,
The trump of God will sound,
And all who love the Lord
Will be homeward bound.

In the twinkle of an eye,
The world will fall into despair.
When God's wrath is poured out,
On all who refuse to listen or care.

In the twinkle of an eye,
We shall shout the victory.
Spared from His judgment,
To complete our Divine destiny.

In the winkle of an eye,
Destined to come our way.
I long for that final blink,
When we will shout, "Hurray"

The repetitive line in each quatrain reveals the location where the action takes place. However, all quatrains discuss what will happen in that place or as a result of the event…in the twinkle of an eye. The central theme is obvious…the return of Christ for those who believe. The supporting verbiage amplifies the central thought with such descriptive phrases as: "The Trump of God", "Shout the Victory", "Shout Hurray" and "Wrath of God".

The title is the repetitive line, a purposeful emphasis of the repetition. The poem builds upon the repetition in an expository manor to look into the central theme.

I seem to have a knack for the use of repetition. I Have several poems that use repetition in a powerful way: "The Angels Cry Holy", "I Saw The Lord", "For The Joy Set Before Me", "He Is Risen", "Galilee Oh Galilee" and "Wise Men Still Seek Him" to name a few.

Repetition drives home the central theme with thought provoking pictures that causes the reader to ponder the idea, to question and to desire to know more.

The Pastor And The Master

If the pastor doesn't follow the Master,
Then I cannot follow the pastor.
But if the pastor walks with the Master,
Then I can walk with the pastor.

When pastors stray from the Master,
The sheep stray from the pastor.
But when the pastor loves the Master,
God blesses the sheep and the Master.

Jesus is the pastor's Master,
And why the sheep follow the Master.
For He is Lord over the pastor.
That's why they call Him Master.

The pastor and the Master.
The Master and the pastor.
The sheep follow the pastor
When the pastor follows the Master.

CHAPTER ELEVEN

Writing Story Poems

Have you ever tried to put yourself in the shoes of someone else and then attempt to capture a feeling of what it might have been like to live in their world? If you haven't, try it. It's a real trip.

Imagine yourself walking on the shores of Galilee with Jesus. See yourself standing at the empty tomb and write what you feel. I have several story poems that were an attempt to capture an event back in time or a feeling of a real or imaginary person. It's a challenge and a lot of fun. I ended up with stories of David and Bathsheba, Daniel and the Lion's Den, Jericho and Me, Samson, Noah and the Ark, Jonah and the Whale and more.

Here are some rules to follow when writing story poems:

1. Make your thoughts his or her thoughts. Speak as though you are indeed Jonah or Noah or other biblical characters. Stay in character.
2. Keep your dialogue central to a particular event or happening that can be woven into a story.
3. Always cause your character to draw conclusions that are moral and meaningful.
4. Make your character bring home the truth of the biblical story.
5. The length of your poem is unlimited but you want to keep it interesting or the reader will get bored.

6. Use lots of word pictures that communicate feeling and atmosphere.

The important thing to remember is that the story has to be believable, biblically accurate, interesting, and always have a clearly presented moral. Here's a story poem for your review and consideration.

Jonah And The Whale

(A story of obedience)

"Go to Nineveh,"
God said to me.
This was while I slept,
In the shade of an oak tree.

Suddenly I awoke
In a terrible sweat.
Chills went down my spine,
And I began to fret.

Nineveh? I questioned God.
The capitol of sorrow,
Where slaves die the death,
Never seeing tomorrow?

Why me? Oh Lord,
I reasoned inside.
I have no desire
To visit that tribe.

But God's Spirit
Continued to speak.
"Go to Nineveh,
It's not what you think."

I said, "Ok, I'll go",
But I was afraid inside.
By the time I arranged passage,
I broke down and cried.

I was too afraid
To obey my God.
So I ran away,
Without even a nod.

I booked passage on a ship,
That sailed at dawn.
Who cares where it went.
I knew I was wrong.

But fear kept my heart,
From doing what was right.
Every time I thought of it,
My skin turned all white.

Shortly after we set sail,
A storm arose that scared us all.
The crew was so afraid,
And their hopes began to fall.

I knew it was God
Chasing after me.
So I told the crew
To cast me into the sea.

We decided to draw lots
And I picked the shorter one.
So they blamed the storm on me,
And settled on what must be done.

So they tossed me into the deep,
That it would calm the storm.
I sunk in the raging sea,
As the ship sailed on.

Sorrow filled my heart,
As I watched the ship sail.
Then, believe it or not,
I was swallowed by a whale.

I tumbled and tossed,
Inside the great fish.
But through my tears,
I began to pray this:

"Ok God", I cried.
"Help me in my time of need.
I'll go to that great city,
With haste and great speed.

Please deliver me,
From the belly of this whale.
I am so very sorry,
That my faith in you failed.

But I'll go and preach
That they will surely die.
I'll carry your judgment,
And tell all of them why."

As I called out to God,
From inside the fish.
I knew He had heard me,
And would honor my wish.

I didn't wait long,
Before God began to act.
He spoke to the whale,
Saying, "Take him back".

With a mighty rush
Of water and slime,
I left the whale,
To proclaim the time.

Dry land felt good,
But I must now obey.
God called me to Nineveh,
To proclaim His Judgment Day.

I raced with the wind, To do God's will.
Now I was no longer afraid.
Instead, I couldn't be still.

There in the city square,
I shouted, "3 days and no more
Your city will surely fall,
And all shall enter death's door."

"God is not pleased
With your violence and hate.
You didn't obey God, And now it's too late."

Then I departed to watch,
For God to seal their fate.
But the people began to repent,
Even though it was too late.

No way, I laughed,
Feeling assured inside.
That city will fall,
Because of its great pride.

But God spoke again to me,
As a friend by my side.
He said, "You repented,
And I turned the tide."

"Should I not do for them,
What I have done for you?
Is my mercy limited,
To only those who are true?"

I sat under a Juniper tree,
Pouting at God's Word.
After all I went through,
I couldn't believe what I heard.

God forgives the wicked;
Whose evil heart cause death?
His mercy is for all men,
Until their very last breath?

"Ok God," I softly said,
As the Lord drew near.
I'll forgive them too
To dry every single tear.

So I went on my way,
Known to all around,
As the man swallowed by a fish,
Only to be returned to solid ground.

CHAPTER TWELVE

BUILDING A BETTER POEM

What makes one poem better than another? Why are some poems rejected and others published? Who decides what's good and what's not?

Bigger Is Not Better

More lines and more words do not mean a poem is better. In fact, some of the greatest poems are short and to the point. The length of a poem is not the measure of one's writing skill. There are several reasons why a poem misses the mark of excellence. They are:

Rambling ... too many poems "Ramble On" never getting to the point.

Sermonizing ... that is to say "Preaching" ... trying to preach through a poem makes for a very bad poem because, it leads to rambling, lengthy text, and a loss of a central theme.

Inaccuracy ... poor use of word pictures can kill a poem. You would never say, "The raging storm is like man riding a bicycle". Typos, improper use of the language, and a lack of proof reading are also killers.

Uncorrelated verses... if you rhyme, your rhyme sequence should not be broken. There is an example of an uncorrelated or broken rhyme sequence:

> Mary had a little Lamb
> Whose fleece was white as snow
> Every where that Mary went
> The lamb was sure to run away

We all know that the rhyme sequence demands that "Snow" be rhymed with a correlating word such as "Go"

Better is Better

A poem that is sure to capture the attention and respect of the reader will display these characteristics:

1. Paints a clear picture of an event or happening.
2. Stands on it's own, requiring no further explanation.
3. Focuses on a central theme that is tied together by correlation of both verse and imagery.
4. Has a "Power Point" that summarizes or brings home the central thought.
5. Employs every day language.
6. Is relevant to the times.
7. Speaks to the heart, not to the intellect.
8. Is broken into stanzas for easier reading.
9. Flows upon a rhythm of metered cadence.
10. Is uplifting and encouraging to the reader.
11. Is a revelation of original thought.
12. Adheres to Biblical truth.

This is a good checklist for self-editing.

A good poem focuses on one central thought or theme. The construction of the poem, using a "Power Point," is to summarize in such a way that there is no doubt what truth or idea is being presented.

To have a central theme is to focus on one thought, feeling, event, or experience at a time. Never mix and match. It will dilute the poem and cause the reader to become bored.

Fragile Flower Red
The Idea

The idea is that we are like a flower, fragile and dependant upon God. We do not blossom for ourselves, but for God, that others may see our beauty and glorify Him.

Quatrain #1… The opening declaration.

As a flower in earthen sod,
I bloom for thee, oh God.
To blossom with the turn of spring,
To be to you, a beautiful thing.

Remember, Do not ramble on or change thoughts in the middle of your poem. Carry through with what you started to say.

Quatrain #2 … This is a correlation of both verse and imagery.

I lift my fragile flower red,
Upward from my earthen bed,
To draw light from God above,
Strength and peace and joy and love.

Quatrain #3… This is the central theme.

As a flower, I blossom for thee,
That passers-by may stop and see.
Your fragrance and beauty I am,

Flowered in grace as a man.

The "Power Point" is the summary that brings home the central theme, so fragile, yet determined to look towards heaven for the power to bloom.

Quatrain #4... The Power Point

**As a flower in earthen sod,
I bloom for thee, oh God.
Upward I lift my head,
As a fragile flower red.**

If we can humble ourselves and judge our own work, we will no doubt grow in our gifting and blossom in the flow of God's Inspiration.

When you are rejected, it is important that you not take it personal. It is not a rejection of you. Nor does it imply that all of your work is sub-standard. It only says that the evaluators didn't feel it was right for them or that your poem didn't fulfill their needs at that particular time.

The final decision

The reader will ultimately decide which poem is better than another. Their criteria for selection can be found in a few simple questions: "Did your poem touch my heart?", "Did it move me to encouragement, faith, hope, etc.?", "Was I blessed in some way?"

You also play a role in the final decision as to what's good or what's not. If you like it, who cares what everyone else thinks? We cannot lay the success of our gifting in the hands of someone else's expectations.

If you have shared your poem with others and they were blessed, any rejection from a publisher should not devastate you.

The poem may be for just one person or a select few. If so, it has already accomplished its purpose. Maybe that's all it was meant to do. Greater blessing through publication is nice but a, "Word In Due Season," to a special friend or loved one is also important.

Don't be discouraged by rejection or comments like, "You can do better". Keep on writing, praying for inspiration and editing your work until you are happy with what you have written. **Let the critical eye be yours**. Look for Originality, Good Correlation, Spelling Errors, A Central Theme, and A Power Point that brings home the message of what you are trying to say.

Our Time Of Prayer

Oh child of God,
Why do you despair?
My angel's camp
Is around you everywhere.

You may not see
My guiding hand,
Yet I am with you
And I understand.

You are troubled,
About so many things.
Your eyes see nothing,
Of what my will brings.

Be of good courage
And walk in the light,
Stand up for the truth,
In the power of my might.

For I love you dearly
And will always be there.
Go now my child,
Until our next time of prayer.

CHAPTER THIRTEEN

Are You Mocking God?

Galatians 6:7 says, "Be not deceived; God is not mocked: for whatsoever a man soweth, that shall he also reap." (KJV) We are deceived when we speak contrary to what God has said. When this happens, we are mocking God.

If we are not sowing what God has said, we will ultimately reap what we say, missing the promises and blessings of God.

How does this thought apply to poetry? I am glad you asked. Whether it's our spoken word or our written word, we are still saying something and are held accountable. If we are not clear on what God is saying, we can inadvertently miscommunicate heavenly thoughts and even end up mocking God.

Mocking God is to say or write in a contradictory manor so as to position your thoughts and written expressions against His. Let me example this for your consideration. Paul wrote to the Galatians; Chapter three. He says in effect…you are foolish for thinking that you can be saved by the works of the law. Who has bewitched you? Good works and strict adherence to the law does not get you a free ticket to heaven, nor does it gain special favor with God. He has concluded all under sin so all can be saved by grace (read Romans 3:3 and 6:23).

The contrast here is salvation by grace or by the works of the law. If we say that we must keep the law to obtain salvation, we position ourselves against His Word and actually mock Him by denying the sacrificial death of Jesus on the cross.

We are actually saying that His shed blood cannot cleanse us from all sin and it will require our righteousness and His to obtain salvation. The same is true if we hint, imply or openly pen a rhyme that conveys this devilish thought. I cannot tell you how many poems I have read that have a flavor of salvation by the works of the law.

Another example of mocking God through poetry is **Pantheism**. We see a lot of "God in Nature" poems. Many refer to nature as eternal with Godly attributes. It is true that the heavens declare the glory of God and that you can see His handiwork in nature, but nature, itself, is not eternal. Only God is eternal.

The written poetic expression is always reflective of what the poet believes. If you believe a certain thing, you will express it in your poetry. That's why it is so important to learn about God and visit with Him often…so you can be true to your gifting and keep from mocking Him in your wrings. The best place to meet with God is in the Bible. It is the inspired Word of God, fully capable of reproof, edifying, instructing, and Divine revelation.

How to keep from mocking God:

1. Keep your poetry in line with the scripture.
2. Read you poem out loud so you can hear what you are saying.
3. Think about the theological implications.
4. Hold your work in light of your knowledge of God. 5. Pray for Divine guidance.

Remember, God is not mocked. That means that He will not allow you to speak or write contrary to His word, without paying the consequences. We will reap what we sow…so let's not offend our Savior by a false confession.

There Is Still Time

Inspired by God's love,
I pen this rhyme.
For you, dear friend,
While there is still time.

Hear my words,
For they are true.
Jesus, God's only Son,
Gave His life for you.

A ransomed soul
On the cross of Calvary.
As a penalty for sin,
That you might go free.

Call upon Jesus,
To give you life anew.
His grace and power
Will see you through.

God patiently awaits,
Your humble cry.
Salvation is yours,
To accept or deny.

CHAPTER FOURTEEN

Profitable Poetry

Do you remember the story of the "Talents"? It goes something like this…the kingdom of heaven is like a man traveling into a far country, who called his servants and delivered unto them his goods. To one he gave five talents, to another, he gave two and to yet another, he gave only one…all to every man, according to his several ability…and then he took his journey. (Mathew 25: 14-30) They were to invest their master's talents and show him a profit when he returned from his journey.

Well, after a long while, the day of reckoning came…the master returned home to discover that everyone did well except the servant that was given only the one talent. He, believing that his master was too demanding and being afraid, hid it or (kept it safe) until the master returned and then gave it back. He was the guy that made his master angry because he did not invest the talent, even in a bank, where it could have gained interest.

The truth in action is really a sharing of authority and the granting of leadership over a portion of the master's kingdom. It was also a test to see if there is loyalty, trust, faithfulness, commitment, and a desire to serve; all wrapped up in a simple request…take what is mine and use it to pro duce a profit.

The word "Talent" in this story refers to money. However, it could as easily have been a gifting from God or several gifts, as the Holy Spirit distributes. There is a clear teaching here that God gives what is His to His own and expects them to use it as though it were a seed, for the purpose of multiplication… so that, when He returns, there will be more than when He left. This multiplication is actually the duplication of rewards and blessings. How do I know this? I know this because our God identifies Himself as LOVE. Love is always kind, gentle and so on. (Galatians chapter 5)

I see this picture in the profile of many poets. There are those that never capture the vision. Nor do they see the need to use their poems in ministry. Some poets want to
keep their poetry safe and refuse to invest it for the benefit of others.

In the story, the good and faithful servants invested their master's money with the expectation of gain, which they could give back to their master. In life, we are given gifts, with the expectation that we are to invest them for the sole purpose of making a profit for the Lord…a profit that shows up in the lives of others.

What is the profit from a poem? Most of us look to a financial reward in the sale of a book or other published work. However, there are other ways to determine the profitability of your poetry.

Consider these:

- Loneliness overcome for a season
- Encouragement for a troubled soul
- A powerful word in due season
- Confusion replaced with peace
- Comfort for a weary heart
- Guidance for the journey
- Perspective for the misguided
- Hope for the hopeless

Money flows through our hands with very little long-term satisfaction and when it's all over, our master will be asking for the profit from that poem or poems given by His own breath. Some of us will be pleased to learn that there were countless thousands that were touched because we invested our time, money and prayers into our gifting. The profit will show up in the encouraged lives of those who read our poems.

However, other poets will have to face the Lord with the fact that they either didn't care enough to invest their time and money for a profit in someone else's life…or that they were deceived in thinking that true profit from their poetry is only seen in self-glory.

Most of us want to share our gift of poetry but do not know how, or what is more likely to be true … **"Most poets are not willing to spend the money to make it happen"**. If you feel I am wrong, ask yourself this question…Have I spent more than $50 to share my gift with someone else? In the last five years, how much money did you put into your own gift?

It has been my observation that many poets do not even have their poetry typed. They sit as **"Anointed Jewels from Heaven"** in a scribbled up notebook. It's time to put up or shut up. It's time to come out of the closet and be noticed. It's time to stand up to the challenge and the responsibility that comes with your gifting. It's time to drop the ego and other attitudes that focus on self-recognition and get on with what God wants you to do. (to be a blessing to others). It's time to stop saying, "I don't know how" or "I'm not a professional", or what ever your excuse is.

Don't be afraid to spend a little money to bless others. It doesn't matter about copyrights, recognition, fame, or anything else. What really matters is being able to stand before the Lord at the end of time and know that we did not waste the gifting He placed within our hearts.

The profit from a poem is the very breath of God being imparted to the body of Christ and other needy individuals. It is an anointed flow of grace that encourages, up-lifts, sets free, and cleanses, producing peace and healing wherever it goes.

We, as Christian poets, are given an unusual gift… to express the very heartbeat of God, as a voice of love to a lost and dying world. How great is that? What an honor. What a privilege. What a joy.

It's time to make a difference, to be different, to enact change.

I will leave you with this ancient Biblical thought…It is for such a time as this, (situation, day, event) that you have come into this place. (gifting, anointing, authority, ability, generation)

God's Highway

(Isaiah 35:8-10)

He places my feet on
A highway called "Holiness"
That leads my soul
To the throne of God.

Amidst the cheers of angels,
I walk wearing His holy gown.
Onward towards heaven's throne,
While evil cast its awful frown.

My eyes were opened
That I might see
Both the good and the evil
That sought after me.

I walk the highway-Holiness
That crosses all of time,
Towards the throne of God,
Leaving this world behind.

CHAPTER FIFTEEN

WITNESSING THROUGH POETRY

Prior to Jesus' departure from earth, just after His resurrection, He addresses more than 500 followers. They were not all apostles. Most were common folk like you and me. His final words went something like this, "Go into your world and preach (proclaim) the gospel (the good news) to everyone. In other words, become a witness of me."

Being a witness, the day-to-day "how to", was left up to the early followers just like it's left up to us today. I guess that's why we see so many different types of ministries. They range from outreach efforts to athletes, nursing homes, youth, to Bible studies, and churches. Its almost as if God's special gifting develops into outreach ministries that testify or witness of Him.

So we, the poets of the Lord, are left with the challenge to become a witness, to proclaim the good news, using the special gifting bestowed upon us by the Holy Spirit. Here-in is our dilemma. **How can we touch the lives of others through poetry?**

    1.   Admit to yourself that you are a Christian poet. Come out of the closet and acknowledge your gifting, even if others do not.

2. Stop looking for approval from others. Write what you feel is from the Lord, even if others think it's bad. The Lord will help you to improve your gift as you use it more.
3. Practice your gift. That means writing often and taking the time to listen to what the Spirit is saying.
4. Look for ways to share your poems to meet the needs of others. That will require a special sensitivity to the needs of those around you.
5. Once you have discovered a need, like a loss of a loved one, depression, loneliness, etc. fulfill it with a "Word In Due Season." become an encourager to the brethren and the less fortunate.
6. Seek out and stay in touch with other Christian poets for mutual fellowship and exchange of ideas.
7. Stay in the scriptures. That means reading the Bible, not as a chore, but rather as a means of communication with Jesus. It is here that you will be filled with faith and also where your spiritual growth occurs.

All of the above suggestions are offered to help you get ready to use your gifting as a witness. The suggestions listed below are offered as ideas or ways to function as a witness, **a shopping list of ideas**):

1. Read the obituaries and send a ministering poem.
2. Send regular letters to the editors of local newspapers in poetic verse that speak to the current event from a Christian viewpoint.
3. Develop your own mailing or e-mail list of friends and relatives for a monthly poem of encouragement.
4. Show your work to your pastor and suggest using it as a resource for church bulletins, newsletters, and in conjunction with sermons.
5. Design short thought provoking poems of salvation. Duplicate them as tracts and pass them out to the unsaved.
6. Take advantage of the holiday seasons like Thanksgiving, Christmas, New Years, Mother's and Father's Day, and any

others you can think of to write a poem and share it with others.
7. Read the wedding announcements and send a poem that fits the occasion.
8. Send regular short poems to the religious editors of local newspapers for use as "filler" copy.
9. Send monthly poems of encouragement to local Christian radio stations for public service airing. Be sure they are short, uplifting, and focused on one central thought.
10. Attend craft, street, and county fairs with a poetry exhibit. I suggest framed poems in all sizes, even as large as a giant poster. This could be a group activity.

The idea to use poetry to witness is actually my vision. It is, as their slogan says, to put **"Poetry In Motion Through Love And Devotion"**, to the glory of God.

Here are 18 more ways to share your gift with others:

1. Become your own book publisher and give it away to others.
2. Frame your poetry and offer them as special gifts.
3. Design your own **"Poetry Newsletter"** for family, friends and selected church members.
4. Make an **"Audiotape"** as a gift item or as a a ministry to the blind.
5. Start a monthly mailing to the religious editors of local newspapers.
6. Mail selected poems to key individuals like political figures.
7. Mass mail your poem thru **Residential Mailers**, like Val-Pak, as a witness to the lost.
8. Have your own **"Poetry Party"** to display and sell your work.
9. Put your work on the Internet with a home page of your own.

10. **"Book Marks"** are great gifts and perfect for resale at shows.
11. Design and frame giant **"Poster Poems"** for your church or office.
12. Write to Christian newspapers and magazines for guidelines for submission of poems.
13. Enter every poetry contest you can with an inspirational poem.
14. Buy the Poet's Marketplace" from a local bookstore and do research.
15. Use your poetry as special occasion **"Greeting Cards"** to family, friends and neighbors.
16. Publish a daily **'Poetic Devotional"**, spiral bound and indexed by topic.
17. Design your own annual **"Poetry Calendar"**.
18. Put your poems of encouragement on designer paper and distribute them to a nursing home.

Why do all of this? Because it's in you and you can't get rid of it. It's a burning fire that compels, demands, and even cries out for expression. That's how you know that you are really a Christian poet…it just won't go away. That's how you know it's of God and not just you. That's how you know you are called to the ministry of poetic expression.

Here are a few more suggestions or ways that a Christian Poet can be a blessing:

1. Put your poetry on a 5" X 7" postcard and mail to all your friends. Any quick printer can print it for you and even do the type if necessary.
2. Spend a little more and include it in the next ValPak mailing to 10,000 residents.
3. Take out an ad in a weekly newspaper with a special poem for Christmas or Easter.

4. Set your poetry to music with an instrumental background on a cassette tape and provide it free to all those interested in your local nursing home.
5. Put your poem on a t-shirt and give them away to others.
6. Make up little pamphlets with 10 or 20 of your best poems and give them away as the Lord leads.
7. Buy an out going tape player and start your own "Dial-A-Poem", giving promo (business cards) to everyone you see, to build a listening audience. This can allow you to change the tape every day, week or month, as you desire.

May our Lord so inspire you and enrich you through His love and grace.

Call Upon The Lord

When your burdens overwhelm you,
Like a mighty raging sea.
Call upon the Lord, Jesus,
And He will set you free.

When your heartaches are many,
And life is difficult to understand.
Call upon the Lord, Jesus.
He will come and hold your hand.

When your friends reject you,
Because you follow after Him,
Call upon the Lord, Jesus.
And keep yourself from sin.

When you fall into depression,
As though it were a giant pit.
Call upon the Lord, Jesus,
Who will restore your joyful wit.

When you're saddened by the day
Feeling lost and all alone.
Call upon the Lord, Jesus,
Who will make His way known.

When you are weary and heavy laden,
Tired from life's many tests.
Call upon the Lord, Jesus,
Who is sure to give you rest.

CHAPTER SIXTEEN

GETTING PUBLISHED

The Big Boys

All of us want to be published. It's a great feeling to have a book in print. Now-a-days, it's almost impossible to be picked up by a big publisher. They do not even look at submissions unless they come from a literary agent. Most poets have already discovered that publishing through these so called normal channels are reserved for well-known personalities. The unknown housewife who writes good poetry has little or no chance to be picked by Zondervan or another big publishing house, especially for a book of poems.

Poetry Contests and Scams

The unknown poet's market is a "Bird of Prey" for many who run poetry contests for the sole purpose of attracting unknowns into a million-page anthology of tiny print poems that is circulated only to poets who spent $40+ per copy and a few libraries.

Here are some ways you can overcome their deceit, greed, and impropriety:

1. Seek the Lord for direction as to what you should do.
2. Establish a battle strategy of ideas on ways to be a blessing and things to do to turn your gifting into profit.

3. Don't be afraid to invest in your own work. You will need to spend a little to get a little. It's a biblical principle of sowing and reaping.
4. Read and do research, at your regional library on the poetry market and how to enter it.
5. Study to show yourself to be approved through books and seminars on your craft.
6. Fellowship with others of like mind where you can benefit from an exchange of ideas.
7. Consider craft shows and other festivals where you can exhibit your work.
8. Identify poetry publishers and send a letter of inquiry as to their publishing guidelines. Your local bookstore can help you.
9. Develop a file of Christian magazines. Call or write for their policy on accepting poetry.

Self-Publishing

Most of us are left with the self-publishing method of getting into print. I did this several years ago and still have books left. The problem with this method is there is no planned marketing or distribution. It takes the big boy marketing to get into the bookstores because they follow the distributor system of purchasing for volume discounts and one little old book outside of that channel messes up their system.

If you self-publish, check out all publishers and get bids to be sure you are getting the best price. Also ask for references and call them to check up on quality, delivery and service.

Publishing On Demand

Watch out for this type of publishing. Most are scams. They lock up your book under contract and publish only as they sell. You have to buy your own copies and they are expensive. They claim big results but you never know if you are getting what you pay for.

Some of these publishers pay a royalty but tie you into the push for marketing among your family and friends, capturing all your list of acquaintances for other marketing offers. In some cases, there are hidden marketing costs if you want more than their initial plan.

I found IngranSpark.com to be the best Print on Demand distributor network. They will work with independent publisher/author types and are very reasonable. They offer a worldwide market and almost every Christian outlet you can think of.

Christian Magazines And Periodicals

The best place to see your poem in print, published, is in a periodical or magazine. However, the competition is tough. Go to the local bookstore and ask for "The Poet's Marketplace" It's a big book that lists all publishers and magazines of poetry. It will take a while to look through it to figure it all out but it's worth the effort.

Web-Publishing

There are many websites that will accept poetry and publish it for the general public's review. Make sure you still own the rights to your poem and that you keep the right to post it in another site or in a book or other form. Then look for Christian radio websites. There are lots of them. Try emailing a poem to them for public service airing, building a list that say they will air your work and set up your own poem of the week, month etc.

If this sounds like a lot of work, it is. But anything worthwhile is going to be work. If you're not up to it, then leave your poems in the bedroom dresser drawer and continue in life as a "Want-To-Be" or you can decide, once and for all, that God really has endowed you with a special gifting that must be shared with others.

The "Way Maker

Only Jesus can make a way,
Through the difficulties of life.
He alone is the Lord,
Over life's sorrows and strife.

He is the "Way Maker,"
When there is no visible way.
He will make the way known,
As though it were the light of day.

He will make a way,
For those of humble heart.
He will clear away the rubble,
Restoring what Satan broke apart.

Jesus is the "Way Maker."
A friend to all who are lost.
He has made the way,
Paying sin's incredible cost.

The way to the Maker,
Is through His only Son.
He alone is the "Way Maker,"
Until life's battles are won.

CHAPTER SEVENTEEN

GOOD POETRY
A "HOW TO" REVIEW

What makes up a good poem? I think it is a combination of several things. It's like baking a cake. If you leave out one or more of the ingredients, your cake doesn't turn out good. So it is with poetry. You must have all of the ingredients to make it good.

Most poets are just average people, not professional poets. They have a gift from God but lack the ability to communicate in a clear, concise manner. I know this because I have reviewed poems for publication and send many of them back for editing.

This chapter is meant to set forth some basic ingredients that will help the novice with their craft. My comments are not an end-all to writing good poetry, only a few personal thoughts that might help.

Now for the ingredients:

A Theme…This eliminates rambling and helps you to focus. When there is more than one theme, it confuses the reader and depletes the power of the overall message. It is good practice to pick a theme and attempt to write your poem around it.

Clear And Accurate Imagery... You would never say, "The tree was like a flowing river" Trees never flow...they sway, and never like a river. If you use imagery, and you should, make it clear and accurate.

A Flowing Rhyme Scheme.... If you are going to rhyme, keep it consistent. That is to say...if you rhyme lines 1 and 3, and 2 and 4 in the first stanza, do it in the second and third and forth also. Don't switch to another pattern in the same poem

A Central Message.... Not only do you need a theme, but also a central message. This will eliminate confusion and help the reader to clearly understand what you are communicating. The message describes the theme and should also be focused to one central thought. Here's an example:

I saw an angel in the sky last night.
He was 10 feet tall, and gave me a fright.
He came with a word from on high
With the answer to my hearts cry.

The theme is, of course, about an angel but the message describes what the angel did. If I were to continue, I would tell you more about the angel and why he came to me, creating a topical theme, in story form, about an angel. When the message leaves the descriptive nature for another thought pattern, it is usually rambling and any real communication is lost. Sometimes the theme is the message but not always.

Let's suppose that I were to continue with the next stanza to do a little rambling:

Then my neighbor asks me true,
Have you a vision or are you blue?
And I responded with, ok.
But God will reign over my day.

I departed, in my focus, causing the theme to shift from the angel and what he was telling me to my neighbor. This dilutes the central message, which is the essence of the poem. This is done often in salvation poems where the poet speaks of the cross and then switches to the plan of salvation or speak- ing to "My Friend" in a sermonizing manner. Your poem should speak for itself in a power packed central message that needs no further explanation.

Proper Form.... The form of your poem or how you construct it is really important. It allows for easy reading. When you are constructing a poem, you should think in rhythm with a cadence. This will make it easier to write it down. Your poem should flow in a specific pattern. You can use couplets, quatrains, or some other form as long as you stay consistant throughout the entire poem.

A Final Editorial Review... Before you let anyone read your work, you should personally review it with an editorial critique. Put yourself in the place of the reader. But before you do that, let the poem sit for at least two days. Then pick it up as though you were reading it for the 1st time. As you read, look for the elements of a good poem: Meter, Form, Theme and Central Message.

Plain Language.... Don't try to become profound by using big words that most people do not understand. Write as you speak, the simpler the words, the better.

Avoid Forced Rhyming... Try not to use phrases that force the rhyme scheme. Let your poem rhyme naturally or not at all..

> There is trouble in paradise
> Where angels do abide.
> There's also joy there,
> That is so very wide.

As you can see, the word, "wide" was selected because it rhymed with the word, "Abide". It rhymes but causes the poem to lack depth.

It actually detracts from any central message. The rhyme has been forced, just to make a rhyme. If you cannot think of a word that rhymes chances are your thought process needs to be changed and editing is required.

Good Spelling… If you are like me, you need a dictionary every time you sit down to write. It only takes a few minutes to proof read your work and run it through a "Spell Check" for

    T   **Y**   **P**   **O**   **S**

Lots of Prayer…all the technique in the world will not make a poem really good. In the final analysis, we need the breath of the Holy Spirit to enlighten us and direct our thinking.

May the Lord bless you as you pen your poems and edit them.

It Came To Pass

Things often come to pass,
But seldom do they ever last.
They come into our busy day,
For a while, then pass away.

We hear their voices, loud and clear,
When they arrive and while they're here.
They speak both joy and misery.
Some to you and some to me.

We say, "It came to pass,"
Or say, "It happened so fast."
Down life's beaten path,
Comes both love and wrath.

So say goodbye to sad and blue.
To all that is now troubling you.
For things will come, only to pass,
But God's love will always last.

CHAPTER EIGHTEEN

WALKING THROUGH THE TITLES

Do you know who you really are? How do you define yourself? What is the essence of you? Most people define their existence by a title. They are a cop, a teacher, a housewife, a truck driver, a scientist, or some other titled walk in life. The title defines them and sets their station in life.

I can remember years ago when I resigned as the Executive Director of a Chamber of Commerce. It was a difficult time, a time when I was just coming back to the Lord after several years of sliding back into the world system and sin. Marilyn asked me a simple question, **"Who are you?"** At that time in my life I could not tell her, because I did not know.

I had, like most of us, fallen into a subtle snare of the devil that led me to define my life and existence by titles. If I were no longer the Executive Director, then…who was I?

Marilyn kept asking me to tell her who I was. You see, she really needed to know, so she could stand next to me in love and marriage. But I didn't know…because I had lost myself in the maze of titles and expectations.

My problem was in how I defined myself. As a Christian, I now know that I am to define myself in relationships, not in titles. Once I saw the truth, it set me free. The title is just a job. But the relationship lives on, growing with every encounter. It's safe from downsizing, economic shortfalls, management changes and other worldly expectations.

We, as children of the living God, are to define ourselves by the relationship we have with Him. Think about that for a moment. Most of us lose ourselves because we do not have a close walk with Jesus. Without His voice and presence, we are lost, only to wander in the maze of titles. He even said, "My sheep hear my voice", yet some would criticize, saying that we are off our rocker because we believe we are hearing from God.

When we define our existence by the quality of the relation- ship we have with Jesus, we realize our true identity and des- tiny. We discover His love, His mercy, His faithfulness, and His plan for our well-being.

Remember what the scriptures say…that we are to be con- formed to His image. (Romans 8: 28-30) Only a relationship with Him can produce that. It isn't found in a title or in book learning. It's in a walk with the Lord.

The term "Christian" was first coined in Antioch, where they called the 1st believers Christian, because they were seen as, "little Jesus". Their relationship with Christ produced the same spirit that was in Jesus.

Paul explains this to us in Galatians, Chapter Five, where he discusses the fruit of the Spirit…Love, peace, joy, longsuffering, etc. "If that same Spirit that raised up Christ Jesus from the dead dwells in us, He will quicken our mortal flesh and make it alive".

What does all this have to do with poetry? Glad you asked. We call ourselves poets, in particular, Christian poets. This can be a title that drags us down and puts expectations on us to be someone that we are not…or it can be a reflection of our relationship with Jesus, empowered by the Holy Spirit for the purpose of sharing God's heart with the world.

We must learn to walk through the titles and allow the Lord to energize us for true ministry. It doesn't matter if we are a housewife, a teacher, a cop or any other profession. What really matters is that we are experiencing a close relationship with the Lord. It's the only way to know that we are loved and accepted. That's what life is all about.

Our poetry should be a symphony of love that resounds inside and flows outward to all around in a Divine statement of our relationship. Spending time with the Lord, in prayer, in His Word, and in quiet meditations of the heart, is the only way we can express His heart to the world. Poetry is a partnership of expressions that is both Divine and human, in one place and at one time.

What title is holding you captive? How do you define your existence?

If you are made alive in relationship to God, by the quickening of your spirit, your poetry will reflect it and no title will ever define your purpose for living. Only God and His never-ending love can ultimately define our existence and shape our destiny. Remember, we are made in His image with the capacity to fellowship with Him and communicate all of what we see and hear. That's the essence of good poetry.

There Is No Other

There's no brilliant light,
Of heaven's newest star.
Only a compelling hope,
For healing of life's every scar.

There are no camels,
Or deserts, windy and cold.
Only God's great love,
And salvation to unfold.

There are no shepherds
To herald His matchless worth.
Only this truth self-evident,
That He came to give "New Birth."

There is no salvation,
In any other name.
Only in Jesus Christ,
Our only hope of fame.

There is no other pathway,
To heaven's throne.
No other name given,
Than His name alone.

CHAPTER NINETEEN

QUESTIONS AND ANSWERS

This chapter is dedicated to questions that were sent in by some of the members of the Fellowship of Christian Poets.

Question... How far should a poet go justifying a problem in rhyme or expression?

If you are following a rhyme scheme, it should be maintained. Dropping out of rhyme to keep the message is not really acceptable. It is done all the time but actually detracts from the flow and poetic beauty of the poem. If you are into rhyme, stay there all the way to the end.

Question... How should we, as new poets proceed, when we have the "want to" but not the "how to" for writing poetry?

"The want to" is the most important part. The technical "how to" will come as you go along. All of us need to practice our craft but if the craft gets all the attention, we loose the power of the anointing. Basic instruction is essential to the composition of good poetry. Knowing how to stay in meter and all about cadence is necessary. Here are some ways to sharpen your tools for writing:

Look for books that teach poetry. In other words, invest a little to gain a lot. Read other poet's work, as many as you can, looking with a technical eye.

Take notes on how they do it and if you like it or not. Then master the technique, making it yours.

Take up a class in your local college or adult education center. Seek out other Christian poets in your area and collaborate with them.

Search the Internet under poetry. There are several websites that offer a dictionary of terms and "how to" articles on the technical aspects.

Question… What is the difference in "freestyle" poetry and poetry that appears to have no "rhyme nor reason"?

Freestyle poetry is poetry that does not have a rhyme scheme but it does have a definite rhythm. If it is freestyle but doesn't have any rhyme or reason, it's not poetry.

Question… Am I good enough to be called a poet?

Good enough in whose eyes? We are not supposed to compare ourselves with others. We seek the Lord, hearing from Him, and pen what we have experienced. The expression will usually come out different in each poet. The style, vocabulary, and viewpoint will usually be different. The true test is in the life of the reader. They ultimately decide what is good and what is not. If they like it, that's good enough.

The gift of poetry, and it is a gifting, is from God through His Holy Spirit. If He has given you the gift, you are good enough. However, as Paul said to Timothy, "Stir up the gift in you". That's the growth process. It takes what God has given and invests it to His glory.

Question… What do I do with my poetry after I have completed a reasonable number?

Go back and review all of them, updating them if necessary. When I look back, I always find ways to improve on what was done before. Then seek ways to use them in ministering to others. See the chapter on "Witnessing Through Poetry".

Question… How do I reach a recommendable blend between biblical and secular orientation?

Most all poets write both biblical and secular poetry. However, I will say this about that. " Where your treasure is, there will your heart be also." If you spend most of your time in the world, worldly experiences and things will inspire the most of your writing.

If, on the other hand, you seek to walk by faith with the Lord, His Holy Spirit will anoint you, teaching you and inspiring your work so it has an impact on the lives of others. Let God inspire you secular poetry as well. Do it all from the eyes of the Spirit.

Question…What if you have written several poems, and then hit a "dry spell" How do you get motivated when your brain is drained?

Dry spells are due to a lack of time alone with the Lord. Remember, your gifting will make a way for you and that way is a partnership between you and the Holy Spirit. Too much time away from the Lord equals less inspiration, thus the term "Brain Dead" or drained.

The solution is; of course, stop trying to write on your own. Get alone with the Lord. When you are there, just enjoy the time and things will begin to happen all around you. It is your relationship with the Lord that makes the difference.

Question…Was there a key event in your life that transformed you into a Christian poet?

I think there is a key experience in all our lives that transforms us into a Christian poet. For me, it was a college humanities class and an assignment to write a paper of some kind. I asked the teacher if I could write a poem. Since I never wrote a poem, I went to the Lord and I have been writing ever since. He gave the gift and the calling all in one request.

Question…How do I know my poetry is good enough to publish?

You don't until you submit it to the scrutiny of a stranger who is probably over worked, under paid and may even have his or her mind on other things. The publishing industry does not focus on poetry, much less Christian poetry, unless you are a well-known celebrity like Billy Graham or some other national leader. The little people like us are left with the "publish on demand" scams or "self- publishing" dilemma, with no marketing outlet or money.

The one true test of quality is the reaction of the reader. If they are blessed and you see a genuine excitement in them over your work, it's usually a good indication that others will react the same. That is the indicator for moving on towards publication.

Question…Should our poetry rhyme? To rhyme or not to rhyme, that is the question.

Poetry does not have to rhyme. There are many good poems that do not rhyme. It's easier to write but, in my opinion, far less poetic…but that's from a rhyme fanatic at heart.

Question…How long should our poems be? How many stanzas?

If your Christian poem is designed for ministry, it should be short, four to six stanzas at best. That is because you are trying to communicate a central thought and using more lines will only encourage rambling. You want a power packed, thought-provoking message.

If you are sending it for publication to a website or magazine, they may have specific guidelines. It's best to find out first before sending in a submission.

If you are not writing for ministry, any length will do, but know that too long is sure to bore the reader. I have poems of more than 20, four-line stanzas, but they are story poems that teach a central truth.

The key to the length is; how much do you need to communicate your central truth or happening? In the final analysis, it's up to you and the Lord.

Question…What is the best way to market Christian poetry?

Considering the fact that Christian publishers, for the most part, invest in celebrities only, I would say the best way to market your work is to create your own sales opportunities. Here's the way I would go about it:

1. Begin putting your poems on designer paper and framing them in various sizes, creating an inventory for use at local festivals and fairs. Focus on seasonal topics, biblical events, dedications, and short thematic poems.
2. Use your Christmas card list as a direct mail list to sell your work, sending them a price list and opportunity to buy seasonal holiday cards.
3. Visit your local Christian and non-Christian bookstores, asking to place your work on consignment.
4. Self-publish your own book and offer it no Amazon.com.
5. Create your own website with an on-line catalog of poems that can be purchased framed or unframed.
6. Create a catalog of poems to mail out to friends.

7. Offer your self-published book to your pastor as a fundraiser in a pre-publishing sale among church members. This will require at lest a donation of 50% of the gross sale to the church as a donation. This will help the church, gain the pastor's support and off set your initial cost. The pastor will need to review your manuscript and could even write the forward.
8. There is always a door-to-door sales effort for the more energetic.
9. Try a classified ad in the local newspaper or religious magazine. This option is a long shot but I'll keep it on the list anyway.
10. Set yourself up on ebay, and see what that does. Millions visit that site every day.
11. Use social media like Face book and Twitter to share your poetry and even sell it.

Marketing is always open to your creativity. Whatever way works, do it. Just keep it ethical and above board.

Question…How much should I edit what I have written without worrying about whether I am going against the Spirit of God's original gift?

Self-editing is essential to creating good poetry. Remember, Christian poetry is a partnership between the Holy Spirit and you. He gives you the revelation and expects you to express it. He wants your creativity, your personality and your vocabulary to mix with His revelation to make the expression. It's a partnership and that's why we need to do the very best to make the revelation a clear and concise expression.

The original gift of a poem should be edited until you have a peace about its final presentation.

Question…Am I suppose to write a perfect poem each time I open my note pad and Bible for inspiration?

Nobody writes a perfect poem the first time out. It usually requires several edits. Now that I have said that, I do recognize that many poems just flow from the throne of God and never need editing. The perfect poem is accompanied by a deep sense of peace that it is complete. However, some times we struggle with the revelation and have difficulty expressing it. Thus the need to edit.

Question…Would it displease the Lord if I wrote a poem, based on a piece of Scripture, from an angle, which was not theologically sound?

All Christian poetry must be theologically sound. What's the point in creating a poem that is off in its biblical message? That will only deceive the reader and displease the Lord.

Question…Should I submit my poetry to non-Christian sites and possibly revel too much information about myself, considering the state of the world?

A Love Poem From Jesus

Arise my love, my fair one,
Come and follow Me,
For the winter is passed
And blossoms are on every tree.

Arise my fair one
Come away with Me.
I long to be with you
Even now until eternity.

Arise my fair one
Come and be one with Me,
For I am the Lord of Host,
Your eternal destiny.

Arise my fair one
Come, give yourself to Me,
For my love is gentle and kind,
With power to set you free.

CHAPTER TWENTY

RESTING IN THE LORD

Remember the big scare about entering the next millennium? What was it that we were all afraid of? Oh yeah, it was the Y2K dilemma, the crash of the computer and a loss of a lifestyle that we all enjoy.

Many of us thought that banks would not be able to retrieve our life's wealth…That grocery stores would run out of food. That time itself would get all muddled so as to lose any sense of normalcy.

Remember the scare that went around several years ago about Jesus coming back? What day was it? I seem to recall September something. I heard that several Christians were selling their possessions and seriously believed that it was all about to end.

And there is always the fall in the stock market, as consumer confidence reaches an all time low. That must mean layoffs, small business bankruptcy, or even worse.

How about a future scare that the Internet will crash, due to too much traffic? All that business and entertainment lost.

Then there are the scares that hit us more close to home like:

1. I may just lose my job.
2. Our marriage is falling apart.

3. I don't know how I will ever pay all these bills.
4. What if I get sick and end up a cripple? Or worse, even die?
5. Thieves could break into my home.
6. My kids might end up in prison or pregnant out of wedlock.
7. Drugs, gangs, disease, sorrow upon sorrow will surely come my way.

These are the cares of this world. These are the things that many of us get caught up in, as we struggle through to make sense of life. But God has not given us this "spirit of fear" that leads us into bondage. He has given us the "Spirit of Adoption", where-by we cry, "Father". His Spirit produces power, and love and a sound mind.

When you are all caught up in the fears or cares of this world, remember that these things do not originate in or come from your Heavenly Father.

Jesus will come back some day and it could be in our lifetime. Will He find faith on the earth, when He returns?

Will He find us trusting in Him to provide our every need?

Will He hear us holding fast to our confession of faith?

Will He see us standing against the devil and the powers of darkness?

Will He be able to say to us, "Thou good and faithful servant?"

I don't know about you, but I want to be all that God wants me to be and to finish the course with joy and a sense of victory, knowing that nothing kept me from the love of my Heavenly Father and the fellowship of Christ through His Holy Spirit.

Like most of you, I am only human. I am forced to battle the fears or cares of this world, just like you. Most of the time, I can overcome but sometimes I too fall short.

My defeats are due to unbelief because I listened to the circumstance, the people around me, and the fear that engulfed my soul. However, my victories are largely due to the opposite of unbelief. It's called faith.

Faith has a way of pulling you up out of the depths of despair and setting you on a plane that is higher than even the clouds. It's as though you were caught up to Heavenly places to be seated with Jesus.

I learned long ago that this kind of faith comes to us only by hearing and that hearing, of the voice of God, in most cases, comes from the literal reading of God's Word, the Bible. I also learned long ago, that the cares of this world, those fears that grip our souls, are only imaginations, cast into a web of deception that comes from the pit of hell.

Paul teaches us, in II Corinthians 10:4-7, that we have weapons that are indeed mighty through God to the pulling down of strongholds.... And that we can actually use the knowledge of God to cast down imaginations and every high thing that exalts itself above what God has taught us.

If you want to get rid of the fear in your life, utilize the knowledge of God against that fear and tell it to take a hike. Here's a practical example…a thought enters your mind, then your soul, that says you will die young due to cancer or some other disease.

The knowledge of God, on the other hand, tells you that Jesus came that you might have life and that life is to be abundant and full. It also tells you that by His stripes, you were healed, a past event. It also tells you that fear is not from God.

There are countless other promises recorded in the bible that will, as you read them, become the "Knowledge of God" and the infusion of faith that will rise up inside of you, as a weapon, to defeat the devil's deceptive ploy to capture you.

It is our choice to exercise faith in the face of fear or fall into unbelief that is so prevalent in the cares of this world. Let us always and from henceforth exercise our faith in Jesus Christ so we can find rest in times of need. The quality of our lives and poetry depends upon it.

Rest My Child

Rest my child, sayeth the Lord.
Take thy peace and be restored.
I have provided thy mouth to feed.
From the beginning, I knew your need.

Do not worry, fret or even fear,
For, my child, I am always near.
To bless thy soul with love and grace,
To be with thee, face to face.

Come, my child, near to my throne.
Do not allow your faith to roam.
For those who will not believe,
Can never find rest in times of need.

My word shall see you through.
My grace I freely give to you.
That you should rest, thy soul to keep
Forever delivered from unbelief.

CONCLUSION

I think by now it has become obvious that writing good Christian poetry requires a close walk with Jesus through His Holy Spirit. Don't follow the path as some who seek the way of the world with all its rules, recognition and fame. This is a snare, fashioned by the devil to keep your gift operating in the natural instead of the supernatural, as God intended.

Your gift will make a way for you, if you give it to God and let Him go before you. Remember, the Scripture says, Mathew 6:33, "Seek ye first the kingdom of God, and His righteousness, and all these thing will be added unto you." The "these things" of Mathew 6:33 are all that the world is seeking after. God will give you all that you need as you walk by faith and not by sight.

May God bless you in your gifting, that your poetic expressions will be a result of being with Him. May His power and anointing lift your poetry to new heights and greater blessings than ever before.

POETIC JARGON

The following is a list of terms that are most common in the world of poetry. I present them as some poetic jargon to be familiar with so you don't look like a complete idiot when conversing with other more knowledgeable poets. A more complete list can be found in the Glossary of Poetic Terms at **www.poeticbyway.com/glossary**. These are but excerpts from that list.

ACROSTIC POEM … A poem in which certain letters of the lines, usually the first letters, form a word or message relating to the subject.

ALLEGORY … A figurative illustration of truths or generalizations about human conduct or experience.

ANTHOLOGY…A collection of selected literary, artistic, or musical works or parts of works.

BALLAD … A short narrative poem with stanzas of two or four lines and usually a refrain.

BLANK VERSE … Poetry written without rhymes, but which retains a set metrical pattern, usually iambic pentameter (or five iambic feet per line) in English verse.

BROKEN RHYME … Also called *split rhyme, a rhyme* produced by dividing a word at the line break to make a rhyme with the end word of another line.

CADENCE ... The progressive rhythmical pattern in lines of verse. It is also, the natural tone or modulation of the voice.

CHAIN RHYME ... Also called *interlocking rhyme,* a rhyme scheme in which a rhyme in a line of one stanza is used as a link to a rhyme in the next stanza, as in the *aba bcb cdc, etc.*

COUPLET ... Two successive lines of poetry, usually of equal length and rhythmic correspondence, with end-words that rhyme.

CROSS RHYME ... A rhyme scheme of *abab,* also called *alternate rhyme.*

DIDACTIC POETRY ... Poetry that is clearly intended for the purpose of instruction — to impart theoretical, moral, or practical knowledge.

EPIC ... An extended narrative poem, usually simple in construction, but grand in scope, exalted in style, and heroic in theme, often giving expression to the ideals of a nation or race.

FEMININE RHYME ... A rhyme occurring on an unaccented final syllable, as in *dining* and *shining* or *motion* and *ocean.* Feminine rhymes are double or disyllabic rhyme.

FORM ... The arrangement, manner or method used to convey the content, such as *free verse, ballad, haiku,* etc. In other words, the "way-it-is-said."

FREE VERSE ... A fluid form which conforms to no set rules of traditional versification.

IAMBIC ... The most common metrical foot in English, It consists of two syllables, a short or unaccented syllable followed by a long or accented syllable.

LIGHT VERSE ... A loose catchall term describing poetry written with a relaxed attitude and ordinary tone on trivial, mundane, or frivolous themes.

LIMERICK ... A light or humorous verse form of five chiefly anapestic verses of which lines one, two and five are of three feet and lines three and four are of two feet, with a rhyme scheme of *aabba*.

MASCULINE RHYME ... A rhyme occurring in words of one syllable or in an accented final syllable, such as *light* and *sight* or *arise* and *surprise*.

METAPHOR ... A figure of speech in which a word or phrase liter- ally denoting one object or idea is applied to another, thereby suggesting a likeness or analogy between them.

NARRATIVE ... The narration of an event or story, stressing details of plot, incident and action. Along with dramatic and lyric, is one of the main groups of poetry.

ODE ... A type of lyric or melic verse, usually irregular rather than uniform, generally of considerable length, and sometimes continuous, sometimes divided in accordance with transitions of thought and mood.

POEM ... A rhythmic expression of feelings or ideas, often using metaphor, meter and rhyme.

POETRY ... A literary expression in which language is used in a concentrated blend of sound and imagery to create an emotional response. It is usually metrical and frequently structured in stanzas.

QUATRAIN ... A poem, unit or stanza of four lines of verse, usually with a rhyme scheme of *abab*.

REPETITION ... A basic artistic device, fundamental to any conception of poetry. It is a highly effective unifying force.

RHYME ... In the specific sense, a type of echoing which utilizes a correspondence of sound in the final accented vowels and all that follows of two or more words, but the preceding consonant sounds must differ, as in the words, *bear* and *care*. Usually, but not always, rhymes occur at the ends of lines.

RHYME SCHEME ... The pattern established by the arrangement of rhymes in a stanza or poem, generally described by using letters of the alphabet to denote the recurrence of rhyming lines.

RHYTHM ... An essential of all poetry, the regular or progressive pattern of recurrent accents in the flow of a poem as determined by the arses and theses of the metrical feet, i.e., the rise and fall of stress. The measure of rhythmic quantity is the meter.

SONNET ... A fixed form consisting of fourteen lines of five-foot iambic verse.

STANZA... A division of a poem made by arranging the lines into units separated by a space, usually of a corresponding number of lines and a recurrent pattern of meter and rhyme. A poem with such divisions is described as having a *stanzaic form*, but not all verse is divided in stanzas.

STANZA FORMS...The names given to describe the number of lines in a stanzaic unit, such as: couplet = *(2)*, tercet = *(3)*, *quatrain = (4)*, *quintet = (5)*, *seset = (6)*, *septet = (7)* and octave = *(8)*. Some stanzas follow a set rhyme scheme and meter in addition to the number of lines and are given specific names to describe them.

STYLE ... The poet's individual creative process, as determined by choices involving diction, figurative language, rhetorical devices, sound, and rhythmic patterns.

TEXTURE ... The "feel" of a poem that comes from the interweaving of technical elements, syntax patterns of sound and meaning.

THEME ... The central idea, topic, or didactic quality of a work.

TONE ... The poet's attitude in style or expression toward the subject, e.g., loving, ironic, bitter, pitying, fanciful, solemn, etc. Tone can also refer to the overall mood of the poem itself, in the sense of a pervading atmosphere intended to influence the readers' emotional response and foster expectations of the conclusion.

VERSE ... A line of writing arranged in a metrical pattern, i.e., a line of poetry. Also, a piece of poetry or a particular form of poetry such as *free verse, blank verse*, etc., or the art or work of a poet.

www.ingramcontent.com/pod-product-compliance
Lightning Source LLC
Chambersburg PA
CBHW020426010526
44118CB00010B/448